# The Art of
# RESILIENCY

## VU TRAN

LifeRich
PUBLISHING

LifeRich Publishing is a registered trademark of The Reader's Digest Association, Inc.

LifeRich Publishing books may be ordered through booksellers or by contacting:

LifeRich Publishing
1663 Liberty Drive
Bloomington, IN 47403
www.liferichpublishing.com
844-686-9607

ISBN: 978-1-4897-3507-2 (sc)
ISBN: 978-1-4897-3506-5 (hc)

Library of Congress Control Number: 2021906677

Print information available on the last page.

LifeRich Publishing rev. date: 04/09/2021

# Contents

# *Dedication*

To all my family members and friends who helped me on a journey filled with challenges, despairs, pains, and suffering.

To my mother, who sacrificed so much in life with the hope that her children would have peace.

To my father, who taught me the values of determination and discipline.

To my teachers, who opened my mind and taught me the skills I needed to fulfill my vision.

To my wife and children, who endure through my failings and mistakes and continue to love and support me.

And most important, to God, who showed mercy and gave me this opportunity to present my gratitude through the hearts and souls of the people I have touched.

Life is a journey of many adventures and discoveries during which we make choices and decisions that may affect our fate and destiny. It was on Good Friday, April 13, 1990, that my life was altered due to a fatal car accident in which I was the sole survivor. The other driver and his passenger, very intoxicated, altered my life forever. I was at the peak of my life with a good career as a senior applications engineer at DSC Communications in Santa Clara, California, and I had a promising future. My fiancée was a senior accountant at Genoa Systems in San Jose, California. We were planning for our wedding around December 1990.

On that fateful day, we were off because of Easter; we went to Carmel Beach. At night on the drive home, I turned to look at her, and when I turned back, I saw headlights coming right at me. In less than a second, my life was shattered. It was a horrific head-on collision; the two in the other car and my fiancée were killed.

The police told me that my contact lens was still on the windshield. It happened so fast that I did not even have time to blink! Just like that, everything was taken from me, including my job because I was laid off a few months later as the Santa Clara office moved.

I followed my fiancée as she was moving toward a bright spot ahead. She turned to me and said that I could not follow her, that I had to go back. I felt a great weight as well as pain; when I regained consciousness, I found myself covered with blood.

At the hospital, the doctor told me that she had died instantly due to a massive brain injury. I felt a great loss and despair as I lay there in the dark emergency room. I heard a loud voice saying, *You plan things, but I make things happen!* From that moment, I knew God had spared my life and given me a second chance on earth to be an instrument.

I thank Michael Minh Đàm, my college buddy who gave me a Bible when he came to visit me after my accident. I thank Lê Diễm-Vân, my family friend and tennis partner who suddenly brought me the cross after I prayed and asked for a confirmation. I especially thank our family friend, Uncle Phạm Hậu, who came to visit me from Olympia, Washington. He came with a message. We visited my mother's coworker and friend who had cancer with only months to live. My uncle took me out to her garden and told me he had to deliver this message to me. He stood in front of me and sang *Kinh Hòa Bình*, St. Francis of Assisi's Peace Prayer: "Lord, make me an instrument of your peace."

As I listened to my uncle, these words penetrated deeply into my heart, and from in my soul I realized that I had just received my life's assignment. From that day, these words became my daily guidelines as I have memorized this Peace Prayer and begin the day with it. I have developed a habit of meditation through prayer, and I have been doing this from 1990 to this day.

Especially when I am driving, I recite a series of Vietnamese prayers such as, Kinh Lạy Cha (Our Father), Kinh Kính Mừng (Hail Mary), Kinh Sáng Danh (Glory Be), and Kinh Hòa Bình (Peace Prayer).

I had received many messages that turned out to be just what I needed to get through the mourning and healing phases. One of the instructions was to write down what I experienced and witnessed to share with others. Up to that point in my life, writing was not my forte, and I really struggled through English classes. I could not write well in Vietnamese, let alone English. However, as I was recovering from the accident, a flow of thoughts initiated neurons firing in my brain, and I just picked up a pen to write continuously in Vietnamese. I was instructed to write a book to share, and it was a process of almost thirty years of living and witnessing God's grace.

I will receive my bachelor's degree in May 2020. It is not for a better job but to open doors. Now I realize that the higher beings did not allow me to gain a bachelor's degree in 1986 or some years afterward but almost forty years later! It has to be at this moment, not sooner, because I have to be a testimony of determination and resiliency.

This achievement has energized me and has made me resilient; I have a message of determination to give to others in this book and in lectures. It will serve as a reminders for others because we human beings do not have much patience just like children don't. People need to know that God has an agenda with the best intentions for our evolution but that at times, we are too impatient or too ignorant to wait for what He has arranged for us. Many times, we try to do things our way, and we eventually run in a full circle before we realize that God's way was the most effective.

Not many people can believe this message. I know nobody in my immediate family believes it because they have seen my failures, mistakes, and weaknesses. My wife is a living witness of all my mistakes and weaknesses. She is my judge as well as my advocate. As a mirror image of me, she has been with me 24/7 and will let everybody know that I am not perfect. In fact, I am a lowly, sinful, and weak person who fails in life. But God can use insignificant and weak human beings to make major impacts around the world. Here is a profound quote from Mother Teresa.

> But I am very sure of one thing: that if God finds somebody more helpless, more stupid, more, more less and less capable and so and so, I think He will do still greater things with her—because the work is His and as He has found me, He will find somebody to do greater things if it is for the glory of His Name.

In one vision, I saw that a tiny piece of ash from a burning bush would be enough to ignite a fire that could light up the world. These words and messages are not from my brain or soul. I have said to my family members and friends that I am only a pen or an audio device and that it would be wise to know who is using this tool and what its purpose is. I leave it to the One who sends these messages to reveal Himself to readers and listeners.

This book is not about ways to become successful or wealthy; many other books offer good advice on that. This book offers a different way of perceiving disappointments, failures, losses, mistakes, and negative situations. When the brain's operating system is updated with this new software to observe, process, and handle such negative data, it will thrive rather than crash and burn.

This book presents the testimony of someone who is searching for a life of happiness and peace, but along the way, he failed in almost everything he did. I do not offer a success story for inspirational support. I wish to share my life story as a road map that contains a lot of failures and mistakes for people to see what not to do in similar situations. By recognizing or learning from someone's mistakes, you will begin to nurture the fruits of failure.

I wish to convey three important messages in my book. First, learning from bad mistakes, major disappointments, and negative experiences is the key to developing resiliency. Second, knowing your purpose or mission in life is the critical element that will enable you to thrive on the path of evolution and survive. Third, I want to establish an alliance of all the survivors and victims who are still struggling or suffering in the darkness of fear, isolation, and pain. Together, our voices and experiences will make a profound impact and be a guiding light for people from all walks of life and especially those who are suffering.

Many people are sinking into despair, isolation, suffering, and torment. They rely on limited, quick fixes such as alcohols, drugs, or suicide. I have heard of too many cases of teenagers and adults who ended their lives because of breakups, cyberbullying, injustice, reckless behavior, and so on. I felt very sad as I imagined myself in the shoes of their parents and loved ones who had to live with the pain through the rest of their lives. When these souls left the physical bodies, they truly sensed the feelings of their loved ones.

They immediately realized they had made a big mistake by bailing out abruptly and shutting down the well-designed programs that were specifically created for their evolution.

By fate, I was fortunate to have been exposed to the spiritual realm during my near-death experience on April 13, 1990. After the accident, I gained a better understanding of faith and spirituality. I was able to grasp the concept that Paul described in 1 Corinthians 13:12, and this is how I interpret it: For now, we are still in the material world so we can only see a partial view of the true reality, but after we pass beyond this world, we will see it face to face. At the present, we cannot fully access the design database with our limited human capacity, but when we leave the physical realm, we will have full access to it just as we had initially. I consider fortune and misfortune, success and failure, as positive and negative events that complement each other by design. An event can have positive or negative consequences similar to the energetic ripple effects that influence our lives economically, emotionally, mentally, and physically to promote growth and evolution.

Nowadays, people's mindsets are so fragile that some commit suicide just because of losing a dream job, or being humiliated on social media, or being pushed by peer pressure, to name just a few reasons. I want to awaken the spirit of resiliency and bring it back into our lives. In the design specifications, our Maker has placed a seed of resiliency in each living creature. We human beings are the sentient and advanced species. All living creatures have remarkable levels of endurance and recovery to survive drastic changes on our planet Earth. The human body has the most sophisticated genetic code. Using my computer language, I refer to the highly advanced operating system (OS) software. It is similar to the recovery mode in our biocomputer's OS software. The spirit of resiliency is not about the strength to get back up after falling or being defeated; it is the ability to dig ourselves out of deep holes or claw our way back from death if you will.

Some people have gone to hell and back; some have successfully weathered their personal storms. They are the advocates and living examples of the spirit of resiliency. They all are inspirational role models who can make an impact on others in their own ways. By uniting our abilities and strengths, we will have a better voice that packs a punch and has impactful resonance. Our collective experiences and inspirational words will become a torchlight that will start a chain reactions in people's hearts and minds. An increasing number of actual testimonies and witnesses will bring others a ray of hope and rekindle the fire of motivation in those who are desperate or suffering.

Our stories and encouraging words can ignite a spark that makes neurons fire to eventually mobilize the nerves and muscles to make this person move out of darkness. Jesus helped the paralytic man, and I use this example to remind myself. To help a man who totally believes he cannot walk, Jesus gives him a ray of hope by declaring that his sins are forgiven (Mark 2:5) because the Son of Man has authority on earth to forgive sins (Mark 2:10). At this point, Jesus has the credibility through the works he has already done throughout the land. Then, to ignite a spark that moves the man's nerves and muscles, Jesus ordered him to get up, take his mat, and go home (Mark 2:11). His voice packed a punch that motivated the man to rise and walk home.

It was by fate that my coworker, John Apollo, told me about Dr. Viktor Frankl's book *Man's Search for Meaning*. After reading Frankl's biography, I realized that each of us needs to help and encourage others to search for and find their meaning of life. As a Holocaust survivor, Frankl actually experienced the painful suffering and faced the angel of death as he was in the concentration camp as well as the death camp. These prisoners had to suffer from painful torture in the concentration camp. When they were sent to the death camp, their fates were sealed because they were about to go into the gas chamber. Frankl was among the very fortunate ones who were selected to work in the death camp. It was a blessing because he became one of the powerful eyewitnesses who gives us the message of hope even from the death camp. I felt Frankl's spirit as I listened to his speeches and read his words. To a degree, I can relate to the experience of the inmates in the death camp who lost everything and walked on earth as living corpses. I can feel their pain when they helplessly watched their loved ones being taken away to be tortured or executed. In my own experience, I described it as the feeling of someone who cut me open and ripped my heart out. I was a walking corpse who had lost all hope and the will to live when I was the sole survivor of that fatal car crash. I was fortunate to receive God's consolation and a vision of what I would contribute with a second chance at life.

I am sharing with you the similar message of resiliency many others have shared. I was moved when I saw Elizabeth Smart's *My Story* with her testimony of courage and perseverance, and Kim Phuc Phan Thi's *Fire Road: The Napalm Girl's Journey through the Horrors of War to Faith, Forgiveness, and Peace* with her path toward compassion and forgiveness, and Hien Pham's account of faith and God's grace as told by Dr. Ravi Zacharias in *Walking from East to West*, to name a few.

I still rely on Frankl's reminders because people really need to find meaning and purpose in their lives. Frankl was among the survivors of the most horrific and darkest history of the human race. Fortunately, after witnessing the horrors of the Second World War, everybody had learned from this ordeal and would not allow the same mistake to happen again. It was the first and hopefully the only Holocaust in the history of humankind. We need to make sure to remind the future generations that millions had sacrificed their lives to teach the world. There are people who had to live through the most tragic or difficult trials to give us the sign of hope, the message of faith, and the strength of resiliency.

I am doing my best to follow the instructions I have received and the chances given to me. I know who is sending the instructions and opening the doors of opportunities. I am only a physical pen or a loudspeaker that God uses to share His words. I can see my journey as a script that God has created with many little stories or testimonies of His grace and wisdom. I am only the author on paper; the real author will make His words come alive in the readers' hearts and minds.

This book is a compilation of many concepts and experiences I have learned. I hope that by learning about my life journey, readers will have a better understanding of their own paths so they can be effective instruments of God. If we become God's effective instruments, He will take care of His useful tools. He will more likely choose the tools that work rather than ineffective ones He often has to fix or make adjustments to. I can relate to this because I have a good pen that always works. I take good care and keep it safe. Whenever I need to write or sign something, I pick this pen because I know it always delivers. In the same manner, we can all become God's effective and favorite instruments.

May God's grace and divine light shine on you as you master the art of resiliency and nurture the fruit of misfortune and harvest golden opportunities.

Vu Tran
September 2019

# PART I

## Chapter 1
# LIFE AND ENERGY

Imagine yourself trapped in the dark abyss of despair, isolation, pain, and suffering. It can cause an awakening to launch you forward, or it can give you a sinking feeling that holds you back or blocks your progress.

I ended up in a black abyss on Friday, April 13, 1990, having been the sole survivor of a car accident. I learned in the hospital's emergency room that my fiancée had died instantly in that crash. That news overwhelmed me; it felt as though someone had ripped out my heart. I totally collapsed. My life was snuffed out, and my soul was taken away. I was thrown into the dark prison of loneliness, pain, and suffering from which I felt there was no escape. I was suffocating because there was no sign of hope and relief. I cried out to God, "Why are you punishing me? You're not fair!" It was my lowest point. I felt I had lost everything.

After the accident, I fell deeper into despair, isolation, pain, and suffering. I hit bottom and decided to take my life. I went through a series of serious suicidal ideations. At first, I thought about driving off the cliff, but a thought came to me—God could easily save me from that crash just as He had done, so I stopped. Then I planned to let the sea take me, but the idea of God sending somebody to rescue me came to my mind, and I had to find another way. On the third attempt, I decided to take a lot of pills and sit in the car with the engine running in my garage. As I was about to start the car, my fiancée appeared and said, "You don't love me! You're so selfish!" I was puzzled by the vision. Then I saw the Lord Jesus Christ, who said, "Just think of all the hard work and sacrifice I have gone through to give you another chance to be my instrument. Why do you give up so easily?" After this message, my mind was clear and my heart was at peace. I began to focus totally on the purpose that God has kept me here for.

Fast forward to the present. I am blessed to have a family—a loving wife and three beautiful children. In 2013, my mother visited us during Thanksgiving and said, "You are very blessed and fortunate to have a wonderful wife and children. Now I think God has a better plan for you when He shattered your life in 1990. I really do not know which life is better. Only God knows. But I can see that you have a very good home right here." I use this story from my journey to share how a person can handle difficult challenges with faith and patience. The aim is to focus on how to bounce back from failure, to stand up again after falling, to recover from deep wounds, and to climb out of deep holes. It is about the art of resilience.

I meditated on this point and went back to a moment that had had a major impact on my life as well as the lives of many others. The year was 1975, and we were at the final stage of the war in Vietnam. In the book *A Vietnamese Fighter Pilot in an American War*, written by my father, Hoi B. Tran, the date of our departure was listed as April 22, 1975 (Tran, 28). I was among the fortunate ones who were able to leave the country before the fall of Saigon on April 30. My father had arranged for us to be on a World Airways flight to the United States. I looked out the window of the Boeing 727 and saw the coastline of Vietnam; I had a sad feeling that I would not see that country again. We landed in Oakland, California, and nine days later, we watched the loss of our country on television. I realized I had lost my home, my family members, and my dear friends in Vietnam.

Many years earlier, when my father returned from abroad, I asked him about the living conditions in the United States, and he told me, "If you ever go to America, you have to remember these two values: hard work and trustworthiness. If you keep these two, you'll do fine." I apply that advice to this day, and I pass on his advice to my children.

After the Black April in 1975, we started to build our lives in the United States with hard work, honesty, and diligence. I had my own challenges because of the language barrier. I was practically deaf and mute because I could not understand what my friends and teachers were saying, and I could not say much to them. I faced overwhelming odds due to personal weakness and a lack of knowledge of my new environment, but I focused my effort on learning and adapting. Eventually, I became a citizen of the United States and adapted to this country's social environment. I have learned that we always root for the underdog.

In Vietnam, there is a common saying, *Mưu sự tại nhân, thành sự tại thiên*, which means, "Man proposes, God disposes." With today's technical and scientific advancements, we tend to believe that we are in control of our destinies. When something goes wrong or something unexpected happens that disrupts our plans, we consider it a failure. We are living in a world of competition; we are taught to be winners, not losers. Particularly in the United States, we see that people are constantly looking for so-called success stories or trying to gain a winning edge. People do not want to fail or lose; they want to learn how to win and be successful in life.

I consider success and failure, fortune and misfortune, as positive and negative energy events. I use the Vietnamese word *Năng Lực*, which means energy, force, or power. However, it does not completely cover the energetic concept that I wish to present in this book. This is a combination of *Năng*, which is ability, capacity, or function, and *Lực*, which is energy, force, or power. Therefore, by saying somebody has *Năng Lực* to do something, I mean this person has the knowledge, skills, and power to achieve it. My energetic perspective implies the combination of information (knowledge) and force (power). For example, by having *Năng Lực* or energy to move a large stone block, an individual knows how to move it and has the strength to do so. Having one or the other is not sufficient; you need both.

Everything exists as energy in one form or another. Each human has a unique DNA sequence, his or her genetic fingerprint. At the base of the DNA structure are cell nuclei that consist of particles such as electrons and protons. The body can also be considered an energetic body. Every radio station has a unique frequency, and every human being has a unique DNA sequence with a unique energy fingerprint.

## Chapter 2
# THE ENERGETIC CONCEPT OF FAILURE

So that I do not have to repeat throughout the book, I use the word *failure* as a general term to mean a disappointment, a loss, or a misfortune.

Using the energetic approach, I look at failure as the condition of an incomplete conversion or an unsuccessful transmission. The cause for this failure could possibly be a device malfunction (i.e., the transmitter or the receiver) or the effects of interference (i.e., noise level or obstructed line of sight). As a result, the intended work or energy conversion is not completed. For example, one morning, I wanted to go jogging, but I was interrupted by a phone call. It turned out to be important, and I spent a long time on the phone. Afterward, I did not feel like jogging and thus did not burn off calories by jogging.

In another scenario, I found an interesting idea that I wanted to share with my wife. I felt excited and could not wait to discuss the idea with her, but she had had a terrible day at work and felt very upset when she got home. During dinner, I tried to start the conversation, but I saw that she was very distracted. Eventually, I gave up because I realized that she could not focus on or even hear me. Therefore, the transmission (communication) was unsuccessful and the data (energy) was not shared.

We can refer to the concepts of radio frequency interference, electromagnetic interference, or radio jamming to understand how communication fails and how data transmission can be unsuccessful. When we are preoccupied, worried, or fearful, we cannot tune in or focus properly. Thus, we are not able to think straight or fully express ourselves. Consequently, we may react in an impulsive or irrational manner due to the influence of interference.

Based on the energetic approach, I give my definition of defeat, failure, and loss in relation to their physical, mental, environmental, and spiritual aspects. From a physical aspect, when we fail to express our intentions or emotions, we can easily be misunderstood and thus become depressed, frustrated, and hurt. An example of this failure comes from a business investment. If your clients misunderstand your motive and cut funding, you can go bankrupt.

From a mental aspect, when we lose our clarity and focus, we begin to have doubts, and we may succumb to fear. At that point, we do not have the inner strength or mental toughness to overcome the difficulty, and we can gradually lose our grip and fall.

When we are in a situation in which everything seems to be obstacles or traps, we can feel that no matter what we try to do, we cannot move forward or improve. Consider a community in which everyone is aggressive, irresponsible, and selfish. Even though we try to be kind, responsible and tolerant, people still take advantage of us and constantly hurt us. If we continue to live in this community, we will not be able to improve our minds and bodies because we are constantly affected by the surrounding negative vibrations.

From a spiritual aspect, when we are totally helpless because we are buried very deep in the darkness of the material traps that cause us to suffer, we do not have any faith or love. We can have all the material elements such as fame, money, and passion, but we still suffer because our souls are trapped and cannot evolve.

I might need $300 to fix my car, but my wife might need $100 for groceries and my son might need $20 for a school field trip. As a result, my car does not get fixed, and that was my goal for that $300. Consider the money as the initial energy to achieve a goal, but things happen that distract me from completing the energy conversion. I have failed due to the fact that I did not achieve my goal, which was to successfully finish what I had started, namely, to fix the car.

After providing the general definitions based on the energetic concept, I wish to present three ways of observing defeats, failures, and losses from material, psychological, and spiritual viewpoints.

First, the material view is quite difficult for us to handle. For example, we can see a defeat as losing face, or a failure can destroy our confidence. We can recover from a financial loss, but the loss of someone we dearly love will be a difficult trial. If we observe those moments and take account of the energetic consequences, we can figure out how the strong vibrations can disrupt or transform our lives.

Second, the psychological view involves the impact of failure on our state of mind. Can we maintain our composure? Are we still in control of our emotions? Do we give up hope? This psychological perspective can help us reexamine ourselves particularly as we focus on our fight-or-flight response.

Third, the spiritual view gives us another slant on failure that could help us turn things around. We may see a failure or defeat as a sign for us to change our way of thinking, to move in a different direction, or to just stop and observe everything around us.

In the United States, we have seen tragic shooting incidents at schools. We have also observed the failure in the system as well as the loss of innocent lives. We need to learn how to console, help, and heal each other. Looking at failures in the system, we can try to fix it. We can let the painful losses of the loved ones affect us either negatively or positively. We can react in a selfish manner, be torn apart by the trauma, and become bitter and unforgiving leading to alcoholism and other negative conditions. As a result, we do not allow the wounds to heal and we continue to inflict more pain to ourselves or hurt those around us. Can we imagine the level of pain and torture we are inflicting on the souls of our loved ones who have passed away? This has a very negative impact. On the other hand, we can live in a positive way, show respect for their sacrifices, and allow their legacies to shine. We allow this love to manifest and last beyond the boundary of death.

By pursuing the concepts of communication and energy conversion, we are analyzing the factors that can determine whether we fail or succeed. In this case, I am referring to the Vietnamese words of *Nhất Tâm*, which means focus, and *Quyết Chí*, which means perseverance. They are the keys that can transform our thoughts or words into reality. For example, a brilliant thought suddenly appeared in my mind when I drove by a sign on the road. Without focus and perseverance, this brainstorm would soon disappear.

In the case of communication, we are not only sending words; we are also transmitting the energy frequencies based on our capacity, which includes learning and living these words. By the application of focus and perseverance, we can raise the intensity of our energy to observe the impact of our words and actions. Actually, we may be able to see the effects as the events unfold in the physical realm.

## Chapter 3
# THE ENERGY CIRCLE

I use the concept of the energy circle, which acts as a protective shield for our overall state of well-being. Think of this energy circle as a balloon that surrounds us. Let me give several examples to illustrate this point. I can rely on my energy circle, which protects my self-esteem and dictates how I interact with others. With a high level of confidence, my energy circle is strong enough to handle the bad remarks or negative criticisms coming from envious people. However, if I lack self-confidence, I will be depressed or hurt when my coworkers mock me. I will be distracted and unable to do my job.

Happiness is another energy circle that each person can create and maintain. It starts from igniting the light of joy in oneself. I think of this light of joy as a candle I want to keep burning in me. I have to constantly guard this candle from the turbulent storms that exist all around me because they could be strong enough to extinguish my candle. The ultimate goal is to fuel this light of joy so it can grow from a tiny candle to a fireball that can spread to others. Many people who are very happy with themselves spread the light of their joy to their family members, friends, and anyone they meet. In this case, we can see how a person can expand his or her energy circle.

Inner peace is an important energy circle that can help us emotionally, mentally, and physically. With inner peace, we can better handle our disappointments and problems. Inner peace is the energy circle that protects my emotional, mental, and physical well-being.

Internal issues such as fear, guilt, and pride damage the protective shield the same way that tiny holes cause air in a ball to seep out. These internal issues are the vibrational points that can create interferences or ambient noises that can attract and absorb negative energies and become targets at the same time. We can use the example of submarine tactics during the Second World War to illustrate this point. Submarines had to be absolutely quiet to escape detection by sonar on surface ships. Applying this concept, we can think of our energy circles as submarines. Our aim is to keep this protective shield intact. As a result, our body will be healthy and our mind will be calm as we sail through the rough oceans of life with many powerful storms and strong waves. Facing internal issues such as fear, guilt, and pride is like undergoing explosions, fires, and leaks in our ships. Such events will raise the noise level and will mark us as targets for ships and invite attacks; when others detect our fear, they will attempt to exploit and control us.

Imagine that we have dripped some honey on our shirt and it is attracting flies. These noise levels or vices will draw attention and make us targets for others. Such internal issues can weaken or destroy our protective shields. Think of a basketball that is leaking air; soon, it will deflate completely and not serve its purpose. On the other hand, if we do not have any internal issues, there will be no holes to allow air out, and our energy circle will remain intact. Additionally, since there is no internal issue, even if others attempt to attack us, there will be nothing for them to hit.

Using these energetic concepts, we can train ourselves to become no-target zones. I am talking about reaching the state of nothingness in which we are no longer the target of attacks. In this no-target zone, we do not send out any vibrational signals that might agitate the energy field and consequently create a feedback or ripple effect. I can use the example of our emotional state to explain this. Let us say I am a self-centered and greedy person. Most of my thoughts and actions will fall within the frequency ranges that include behaviors such as aggression, destruction, insensitivity, provocation, and recklessness. Inevitably, the people around me will react to these vibrations, and the events that happen will be the results of what I have created.

I have learned by meditating to see everything beyond good or bad, high or low, and right or wrong and adapt the nondualism or monism rather than a dualism framework. I have reprogrammed my brain's central processing unit (CPU) to see good and bad, high and low, and right and wrong as one. I have rid myself of many negative data stored in my memory. For example, when I hear a negative remark from somebody at work, if I allowed the brain's CPU to analyze the data as bad or negative and save them, I would be saving and accumulating a lot of negative data. As a result, these negative data will cause me to feel emotionally unstable, upset, and depressed.

Many people are easily convinced, deceived, influenced, and misled and become instruments of destruction. People can be greatly affected by hatred and violence. I refer to the hate virus or H-virus to make my point. The H-virus can spread quickly and cause painful suffering in the network of human lives. It has a wider range than infectious bacteria, deadly germs, and airborne pathogens have because this virus can spread quickly with just a click of a mouse or a cell phone and go viral on the web. We have seen how teenagers can be driven to suicide because they could not handle the hateful or threatening messages from cyberbullies. People can be brainwashed by the H-virus to become aggressive, irrational, selfish, and violent. We live in a volatile environment in which anything can be flammable or explosive. We have seen too many news reports about abused children, domestic violence, hate crimes, road rage, and terrorist attacks. Each such incident is a teardrop that will eventually fill up the container of human tears. When the last teardrop makes the container burst, it will cause a major shift in the cycle of human evolution. There will be many changes in the way we think, act, and live.

I need to strengthen my energy circle to help myself as well as those close to me. On rainy days, we put on raincoats and use umbrellas. When we face storms in life, we need psychological, emotional, and spiritual raincoats and umbrellas. I offer my knowledge of the energy circle as a raincoat and umbrella to those who have nothing to cover themselves with.

Regarding the energy circle, we can apply the God-presence energy or GPE meditation technique to train ourselves to be in the state of nothingness. We are talking about reaching the condition of total emptiness or nothingness in which we can no longer be the target of attacks. In this context, it involves all the frequencies of energy vibrations around us. In this state, we do not send out any vibrational signal that might agitate the energy field, which would consequently create a feedback or ripple effect.

Along with clearing all our negativities, we also need to consider the impact caused by holding on dearly to something or someone we love. When we hold onto something very tightly or too dearly, it becomes a part of us and eventually becomes a potential target. This mindset of holding on can be one that blocks us, distracts us, slows us down, or stops us. When we struggle with many problems or difficult trials, we need to face the painful truth. Sometimes it is hard to acknowledge that the root of all these problems is those we love the most—mother, father, brother, sister, son, daughter, husband, wife, lover, or sweetheart—who create conflict, distraction, envy, headache, heartache, pain, and suffering. They can block our path, oppose our cause, rattle our cage, or sink our boat. These are the strong vibrations that can weaken us or make us vulnerable to all kinds of physical, mental, and spiritual attacks. This is one reason we constantly have difficult problems, drawbacks, and failures.

When we practice self-cultivation and purify ourselves of our negativities and vices, we are running the software to clear the bad vibrations in ourselves caused by others that damage our energy circle.

## Adverse or Favorable Conditions

Adverse conditions can alter or block us from reaching our goals while favorable conditions can help us achieve our objectives. These factors can take the forms of our emotional state, family support, financial status, health conditions, and timetable. Aircraft can be helped or hindered by tailwinds or headwinds. I use the Vietnamese concepts of *Nghịch Duyên* or opposing circumstance and *Thuận*

*Duyên* or favorable circumstance to present this point. Under opposing circumstances, we have to spend more energy to deal with the challenges, obstacles, and problems, and sometimes we may not be able to reach our goal. Under favorable circumstances, everything seems to be in alignment and we reach our destiny with ease.

Let us say an employee needs the manager's approval to put his idea to work. A selfish manager will let his ego get in the way of helping his employee; the manager is an opposing circumstance that the employee will have to expend more time and energy to overcome if he wants to carry out his project. An understanding and supportive manager in this case would be a favorable circumstance. Using the energetic concept, we can either create headwinds or tailwinds with the vibrations of our thoughts, words, and actions.

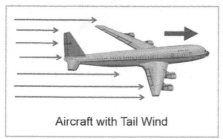 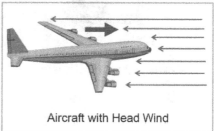

| Aircraft with Tail Wind | Aircraft with Head Wind |

Aircraft with a tailwind or a headwind

## The 70/30 Scale

We can consider the following scales to measure the overall growth and efficiency of an organization.

Result: no learning, no progress and no evolution

**100/0**

Here, we are looking at 100 percent pro and 0 percent con, the worst-case scenario because in it, there is no challenge, opposition, or questioning. When the leader says, "This is A," everyone agrees it is A and nobody challenges his view. Therefore, people will close their minds and blindly follow their leaders or their ideology. Consequently, this path may lead to totalitarianism or monocracy. Throughout history, we have seen political leaders and rulers who eliminated all their opposition to gain absolute power with 0 percent resistance.

Result: Clashes, division, friction, gridlock, stagnation, etc.

**50/50**

Here we have 50 percent pro and 50 percent con, not a healthy scenario. On this scale, there is constant struggle in the organization and it cannot grow; equal but opposing forces stop any movement.

Result: Spawn healthy progress, improve
quality, promote evolution, etc.

## 70/30

Here we have 70 percent pro and 30 percent con—the best-case scenario. With a majority of people willing to move forward, we also need people who challenge or question us. This 30 percent of challenge, opposition, or questioning is the fuel to stimulate growth while serving as a check and a balance.

Resiliency helps us dig our way out of the deep holes we can occasionally find ourselves in. When I came to the United States in 1975, I had to restart my life from ground zero and learn a new culture and language and ways of interacting socially. I took my father's advice and was hard working and trustworthy, and in 1990, I was a senior applications engineer with a promising future.

When I lost everything in that horrible crash, I felt that I had been buried alive and was suffocating emotionally, financially, and mentally. My pain was so unbearable that I could not cope with my normal routines. I lost my job and did not have the will to go back to work. As a result, I began to sink deeper into poverty and was almost homeless. Mentally, I was in total darkness and thought of ending my life. Though I was in utter despair, a voice from the depth of my soul kept reminding me, *God brings the storm to you, and He also guides you back out to the sunshine!* This soft voice encouraged my heart and mind as I steadfastly endured through the desperate and suffocating times. Gradually, I found myself clawing my way out of a very deep hole. It took me from 1990 to 2020 to get out of that pit of hopelessness. I endured the process and felt like a scout that maps unknown lands for the benefit of those who follow him.

PART II

## Chapter 4
# THE HEAVEN-EARTH-HUMAN FACTORS

Based on the energetic approach, everything exists as energy including space and time. We can consider an event that happens in space and time as a form of energy or work. For example, we can have an idea that we spend time and energy on to bring it to fruition. A composer goes through this process all the way from putting notes on paper to finding musicians to practice and play all the parts of his score on a special day, when all the pieces come together to the delight of the audience. This is energy being converted by an idea in the form of thought waves to music, sound waves. This is then transformed into the feeling of joy, an emotion. If the composer, or conductor, or a musician fails in one respect or another, the energy conversion or transmission does not take place completely and the audience might not feel as satisfied or happy.

I use this example to describe the elements of heaven, earth, and human. In Vietnamese, we refer to the elements of heavenly timing, earthly advantage, and human harmony. We can describe heavenly timing as our destiny. Sometimes, a certain event happens precisely at a particular moment, not earlier or later. As we reflect on such events, we can see that these moments happened with perfect timing or perhaps were predestined. We can define the earthly advantage as the environment, where an event takes place.

Let us go back to the example of the musical score above. Without the right concert hall equipped with the proper acoustics, the audience cannot clearly hear all the music and therefore cannot fully enjoy or appreciate it. Finally, we can draw a comparison between human harmony and the mind. In this context, we are talking about the collective mindset of a whole group as everybody agrees and works together. From the example of the concert, the instruments play together in harmony to fully radiate the beautiful sounds. This delivers the essence of this musical score as the composer had intended.

Let us examine how you can apply this concept of heaven-earth-human in your daily life. When something happens to you, you need to remind yourself of the heavenly timing element and whether the situation is good or bad. You accept that it had to happen at that exact moment, not yesterday and definitely not an hour later. If it is a bad situation, you might ask, *Why now? Why me?* But if you think deeper and raise your level of consciousness, you will observe the whole situation with a calm and open mind. Therefore, you will gain a better understanding that will help you find some clues that will help you realize why it happened.

As we live and learn, we gradually pick up pieces of information through all the good and bad experiences. Eventually, we will reach a point that allows us to put these pieces together and begin to see the big picture. This is when we recognize that we have attuned ourselves to the heavenly timing factor. When we first drive an unfamiliar road, we pay attention to our route, which will make it easier the next time we drive that road, and we will no longer be anxious about it.

Not being able to see anything at night, pilots depend heavily on instruments to navigate; they do not allow themselves to be distracted by anything else. If we pay attention to everything that happens around us, our instrument panel, we can record and remember all the signs including warning signs before something bad happens. It may be precognition or perhaps déjà vu.

People often want to gain an edge while making decisions and will even consult fortune-tellers and psychics to tell them the future. In Vietnam, people regularly visit fortune-tellers and psychics during the lunar New Year to know what lies ahead, or they attempt to read the prophecies to find some clues.

We can consider prophecies as the design specifications of a system that describe how the system would work in various scenarios. Therefore, we may predict what will happen to the system if we do a certain thing to it. On the other hand, we can think of the book of prophecies as a road map to chart our course of action. We can read these warnings and visions as signs that will help us make better decisions or change our course to avoid dangers and problems.

If people can recognize signs and learn from warnings to improve their level of consciousness, that will help them modify the whole system. Prophecy can be viewed as a road map that allows you to take precautions or change direction. If you are so distracted that you do not see these road signs, you may run into problems and danger.

People have craved control of time throughout history so they could see the future and acquire immortality. One of the most powerful and distinctive people in history was Qin Shi Huang[1] (259–210 BC), the first emperor of a unified China. During his reign, he wanted to find the elixir of life, which supposedly would allow him to live forever, but he never did. He wanted to be immortal so he could rule forever.

The earthly advantage element is our environment. It may be a favorable and harmonious atmosphere or circumstance, or it may be where we live, learn, or work. The earthly advantage element includes our physical well-being and management skills; it is a profound concept. It is not the literal meaning Vietnamese people often think of—that with fame, money, or power they can attain it. You can use fame, money, and power to gain an advantage in the physical world, but that is only a small part of the earthly advantage element.

A famous and wealthy businessman who wishes to obtain the earthly advantage element might purchase a state-of-the-art office building and offer his employees pay raises and bonuses to motivate them, but some employees are not motivated by nice offices, raises, and bonuses; these elements are distractions more than motivators. They will move on if and when something better comes their way.

---

[1] http://asianhistory.about.com/od/profilesofasianleaders/p/qinshihungbio.htm.

It takes more than fame, money, or power to achieve the earthly advantage element; it also takes management skills. With good management skills, you can create a friendly and productive working environment in which all the employees feel good about themselves and their jobs. We can see this earthly advantage component from another angle by referring to the common Vietnamese saying *Xây tổ ấm*, "Build a warm nest." We want to create a loving, happy, and warm atmosphere for ourselves and others, and that takes more than fame, money, and power both at home and at work.

I use the energetic principle to describe a balanced and harmonious field of energy in our homes. Indeed, most of us focus all our time and effort on creating the proper energy field in our home. We pay attention to every detail and make adjustments and corrections to the atmosphere and our interactions. We express caring, loving, and supportive energy to open the lines of communication, to improve our relationships, and to create joy at home. Everybody feels good and helps build and maintain this loving, warm household. We may not be famous, influential, or rich, and we may not live in a mansion, but we can feel love and warmth in our small homes. We can generate an energy field that benefits and nurtures the members of our families.

On the other hand, we may be very popular, powerful, and wealthy but not have feelings of love or warmth at home because we have not devoted the time and effort necessary to build the foundation; we only try to buy it. We pay others to clean our house, cook our meals, take care of our garden, and so on. Sometimes, we do not even know where to find certain utensils because we were not the ones who put them away. From an energetic aspect, we do not establish a connection with the energy field in our home. Our home is more like a hotel, an external shelter but nothing more.

We may have experienced this sensation when we were invited to a party at a friend's house. Even though the house was expensive with all the luxuries, we did not feel a warm, loving atmosphere there. Sometimes, we do not feel joy or happiness at home and thus try to find it outside home. We can throw a party to get people over, but it is only the exterior, and the good times disappear as soon as all the guests are gone. We can apply this concept of the warm nest to our homes no matter their size and on a larger scale—to corporations, communities, and societies.

The human harmony element includes our inner peace and the way we interact with others. The first facet is quite straightforward; it deals with our state of well-being, inner peace. If you do not feel well or do not have inner peace, you may not be as tolerant of your friends and family as you would be if you were healthy and happy. We need to achieve a sense of well-being if we want to improve our lives and calm our minds.

The second part of the human harmony element concerns the way we interact with others and how we can influence them. We may need to develop the proper communication capabilities, leadership qualities, and management skills to do so. It may be necessary to develop an open mind and spiritual insight. How can we reach out to others and expect them to understand our ideas if we cannot communicate well with them? How can we set an example for others to follow if we cannot do everything we ask them to do? How can we function in an efficient and professional manner if we cannot do that ourselves? We need good hearts and souls, but without the human harmony element, we will not have them. We would be eye-catching but empty bottles of wine.

We need to be mindful and take care of ourselves if we want to be more presentable. We are not talking about taking extreme steps to look beautiful or buying expensive outfits; we are talking about our true appearance that includes things like our health, actions, thoughts, and words. We see people who may have good looks, but the way they act or treat others can turn people off and completely destroy their image. We should focus on how to gain people's respect by respecting ourselves first. If we can show a sense of responsibility and respect toward our own bodies and souls, people will see this and respect us. In Vietnamese, there is a saying *Tâm phục khẩu phục*, "Respect in the mind, respect with the words." When people totally respect you, they show a deep sense of respect in their minds because they think of you as a role model. These people also express the respect with words, as they always speak highly of you.

*Tâm phục* can mean that people deeply respect you in their minds and hearts and will follow you. *Khẩu phục* can mean that people are proud of you and will support you. Naturally, you cannot gain this level of respect with fame, money, power, or intellect. People may be impressed with you or intimidated by you, but they do not respect you. Imagine a group leader who orders his team to march ten miles but is very obese and cannot walk even one mile. The team members have to obey the order because of the leader's rank, but deep inside, they will not respect this leader.

If a mayor of a small town facing an economic crisis tells everyone to cut back on spending but continues to hold extravagant parties, he will not earn the people's respect and will not experience human harmony. If we are aware of our vices and virtues and respect others, we will have the human harmony factor on our side.

We can draw a parallel between the heaven-earth-human factors and the spiritual-material-psychological factors. The heavenly timing can relate to the spiritual cycle that benefits the soul. The earthly advantage can relate to the material environment that benefits the physical resources. Human harmony can relate to the psychological state that benefits the body and mind. The union of these three factors can benefit our spiritual development, physical well-being, and mental calmness.

By using the energetic approach to combine heavenly timing, earthly advantage, and human harmony, we will have full control of our destiny. We will find ourselves in the right place with the right people at the right time. Since we are fully aware of this alignment, we will send out energy signals in the form of thoughts, words, and deeds. It will be powerful because the energy transmission or conversion will be completed.

By contrast, if you are distracted or anxious and ignore the alignment of these three elements, meaning that you attempt to execute a plan too soon, are not in a suitable environment, or do not have the right people with you, you will not be able to achieve your objective. You will have wasted energy because all your effort and time was spent without any fruitful results. Therefore, the energy transmission or conversion was not completed.

We can use the concept of a three-legged stool to help us remember the alignment and balance of the heaven-earth-human elements that will contribute to our success. If we are missing any of these three legs of the stool, we will likely not achieve our goals. If we want to grow tomatoes, we need seeds and fertile soil with the proper nutrients and we have to tend the plants. Without any one of these factors, we will end up with no tomatoes. We cannot cut corners here just as we cannot cut corners when we develop a plan to achieve something.

If factors such as culture, tradition, family, and society cause us to bargain or compromise, we may not have the proper atmosphere to implement our plan. Also, we need right people to harmonize with to allow us to do the work and complete the tasks. However, if we are distracted or blinded by fame, fortune, and fornication in the selection process, we may not have all the right people for the job and there will be internal problems and conflicts.

We have many examples of sages and leaders who seemed to have everything supporting them; they had the favorable elements of heaven-earth-human to help fulfill whatever they attempted to do despite the odds they at times faced. Ordinary people typically consider their achievements as marvels or miracles. In Vietnam, parents and teachers repeatedly remind their kids, *Có chí thì nên*, "Where there is a will, there is a way." We may have the will, but we also need supporting heaven-earth-human influences as well.

Let's say I have a talent for designing fashionable clothes and a strong will to succeed in the retail business. I have the willpower and determination to stick to my plan. However, I do not have the three elements behind me, and consequently, I will go through life without achieving my goal. I do not have heavenly timing, so it happens to be in the middle of the worst economic and political crisis in my country. I do not have the earthly advantage because my land is ravaged by crime, riots, wars, etc. And I do not have human harmony because people are focusing on survival, not fashionable clothes.

Along with sufficient willpower, we need compassion, wisdom, and courage. If our willpower is combined with compassion, we can interact with, tolerate, and understand people better. If our willpower is combined with wisdom, we will be better observers who will know when it is the right time to react and to start something. If our willpower is combined with courage, we will have the patience to endure challenging and difficult environments.

Let us suppose that we have the timing factor, the environment is favorable, and all the right people come together. For example, let us say that we run a computer company, and we determine that it is the right time to develop an artificial intelligence system that emulates the human thinking process to interact with the users, what we refer to as the complementary brain. We find a manufacturing plant that can build the parts, so we have a favorable environment. We also have engineers and technicians who know how to put the design together. In all, we seem to have a good concept, a favorable environment, and the right people, so the outlook is promising.

However, as we plan the designing, manufacturing, and selling phases, human intention begins to play a role. Each person may have a different intention, and these various objectives will slow down the project or in time alter the plan. When we refer to the human intention, we are trying to emphasize the critical key—harmony. In this scenario, if all the engineers and technicians focus on one common intention, which is to build the system, they will be able to look beyond their differences and conflicts. We can categorize these conflicts and differences as the glitches in the system, interfering distractions.

If we use the energetic approach to observe all the events and interactions that happen around us, we can see that when the three elements are formed, an idea, event, or plan will take place. It will not occur if we are still missing one of the three elements. It will not have the energy necessary for it to materialize and become reality. We can use a common Vietnamese phrase to help illustrate this point: *Có công mài sắt có ngày nên kim*, "Diligence is the mother of good fortune."

## Chapter 5

# RANGER'S STORY

Ranger is the name of my daughter's stuffed dog we bought for her when she was two. She loves Ranger very much and carries him with her everywhere. She is twelve now, but she still takes good care of Ranger. Over the years, Ranger became a part of our family because my daughter took him even on vacations.

While I was meditating one time, I found myself in Ranger's place, and it revealed a meaningful message. I imagined myself being in the toy universe, and compared to the other toys, he seems to be well treated by the human gods. As long as they still love Ranger unconditionally, he continues to be blessed and protected even when he does nothing. On my daughter's twelfth birthday, her friend came over, and they were playing with all the stuffed animals. When they were playing a little rough, my wife said, "Girls, leave Ranger alone! He's fragile." The girls listened and placed Ranger on the couch.

Ranger is loved by the human mother god, and even her human angel daughters cannot harm him. This particular scenario suddenly reminded me of Job's story in the Old Testament when Satan wanted to test his faith. God specifically told Satan to test Job but not kill him (Job 2:6).

Many times, we believe we do not deserve God's love because we have not done anything good or we know we have disobeyed Him. Regardless of our circumstances, God loves us unconditionally and continues to find ways to bless us. However, at times, we do not recognize God's blessings because we are too distracted, ignorant, or overwhelmed by our issues. But when we are calm, we begin to see how God's subtle hands have saved and touched our lives. In my mind's eye, an inanimate object such as Ranger becomes a reminder of God's love and grace.

God works in mysterious ways, and nothing is impossible for God. Whenever I face negative or stressful situations, I remind myself of how God used Ranger to bring happiness and peace to a little girl who would eventually extend the love to unite our hearts. If God can do this with an inanimate object, rest assured that He will do a lot more with us.

Through the years, I have watched all the *Toy Story* movies with my children, and now, we have Ranger's story to pass on as a profound reminder of the alignment of heavenly timing, earthly advantage, and human harmony that God has allowed to express His love for a little girl.

## Chapter 6
# GOLD'S GYM STORY

After my car accident in 1990, my doctor told me that it would take me many years to really feel the impact of my injuries. About five or six years later, I began to have constant pain in my neck and lower back. I have learned and practiced meditation to help myself. I also took my doctor's advice and watched my diet because excess weight may cause more damage to my joints and bones since I was already injured.

It was by fate that my brother-in-law happened to join a Gold's Gym and offered to sign me up on his family membership. I have been a member for more than ten years now. Each day, I go there and exercise by doing push-ups, sit-ups, stretching, and meditation in the dry sauna. After night shifts, on my way home, I usually stop by the gym to exercise and meditate in the sauna. By the time I arrive home, I have already finished my daily exercise and have showered.

A day after a bad snowstorm, I went to the gym and the staff said, "We're glad you could make it!" At first, I did not think much about that because it was something I had heard many times. However, when I was meditating in the sauna, I received a wonderful thought. I imagined the gym as a place with a special atmosphere that each person must have a certain capacity of to enter. They must want to improve their health, and they need a disciplined routine to do that and not be distracted from achieving that. People who go to gyms regularly have workout routines, and they encourage other gym goers. Their presence and perseverance definitely motivate others.

One time, I had a vision of a golden castle. I went in it and found myself in a different atmosphere and condition. The castle was covered by the light of joy and the field of harmony. All the people there had reached a level of consciousness and created the light of joy. The residents developed their living standards, and the castle was a happy, peaceful, and stress-free place.

Some have to fight our way through the emotional, mental, physical, and spiritual challenges to get to the gate. Others need guidance or help to make it to the gate. Eventually, when we enter the golden castle, we realize that everyone there is happy, peaceful, and stress-free. It takes a tremendous amount of discipline, willpower, and hard work to get out of adverse circumstances, difficult conditions, and tough situations to get to the golden castle.

The castle represents a collective field that includes the energies of self-control, positive mindsets, good attitudes, physical health, and inner peace. These energies come from those who live there. This is another way for me to remember the heaven-earth-human factors as we are at the right time and have arrived at the right place and have met the right people, so the combined energy field is very strong.

# PART III

## Chapter 7
# ADVERSITY BRINGS WISDOM

Each day, we have to deal with many issues and problems as part of the normal condition of living. We know we will have to confront challenges and overcome adversity, and we prepare ourselves for the daily battle. We need all our energy and wisdom to make decisions and act accordingly. At the end of the day, our decisions and actions may affect our state of well-being, our family members, and our living environment.

If we have a condition such as chronic arthritis, we will struggle every day. If we are overwhelmed by our work responsibilities, we will have to encourage ourselves to focus mentally to tackle our tasks. We can suffer emotionally if we are tormented by the memories of a loved one we have lost. To fight our daily battles, we need to know our capacity and the opposition's strength whether we are dealing with a business, family, or personal issue.

We can reference a well-known concept from Lionel Giles's translation of *The Art of War* by Sun Tzu.

> If you know the enemy and know yourself, you need not fear the result of a hundred battles. If you know yourself but not the enemy, for every victory gained you will also suffer a defeat. If you know neither the enemy nor yourself, you will succumb in every battle. (Giles, 11)

The first part of this advice is to know yourself. This does not mean your physical strength, intellect, social network or wealth; it means knowing your true self—who you are and the meaning or purpose of your life.

The second part is to know your enemy. Let us apply the principle of the heaven-earth-human factors to survey the opposing sides. If you know a problem exists in the network system of the office building where you work, you need to know exactly what the problem is to determine its cause. While applying the principle of the heaven-earth-human factors, you first look into the timing issue. Perhaps the fileserver's software needs to be upgraded because it reached the maximum number of users, or maybe the disk is almost full. Next, you check the environmental factors. Perhaps the wire cables are damaged since you added more cubicles, or maybe the hubs malfunctioned. Finally, you examine the human factors. Perhaps someone accidentally downloaded a virus that damaged the operating system, or maybe a hacker has taken over the network. We can see how to apply this timing-environment-human concept to deal with a network problem.

We look at adversity and challenges as the enemies that can attack, destroy, disrupt, and transform our lives. We need to distinguish between friend and foe, between good and evil. We want to look closely at how we define good and evil. Something good can be constructive, useful, and beneficial for us and others, and anything evil inflicts pain, suffering, and destruction or causes catastrophic consequences to one or more people. In our modern, complex world, the way we define good and evil can be influenced by religious, spiritual, political, and social factors.

From the birth of Christianity until now, the church has had absolute power over nations and people. This was especially true during medieval times. Christians who defied the church would be condemned as heretics and excommunicated. Throughout history, the church has arrested, condemned, and executed people on charges of heresy or belonging to cults. In many cases, the church was forced to make such accusations due to economic, political, and social influences.

Many years later, however, the church changed its position. For example, during a conflict between England and France, the church condemned Joan of Arc (1412–1431)[2] after she was arrested for being a relapsed heretic, and it burned her at the stake in 1431. Twenty-five years after her execution, she was exonerated of all guilt. She was canonized in 1920, and she is now regarded as the patron saint of France.

Galileo Galilei (1564–1642)[3] was arrested and charged with heresy. More than three hundred years later, on October 31, 1992, Pope John Paul II gave an address on behalf of the Catholic Church in which he admitted that errors had been made by the theological advisors and declared the Galileo case closed.

In Buddhism, as in other religions, many followers live in a state of false reality or illusion because they are misled by monks who misinterpret or misunderstand the teachings of the Buddha. This misunderstanding leads some Buddhists to believe in total detachment from the physical world as a way to reach Nirvana. The law of karma plays a central role in bringing fear into the minds of Buddhists. This illustrates that the definitions of good and evil may differ between religions.

For example, Christians believe that the only way to salvation is through faith in Jesus Christ since the Lord had already paid the ultimate price to redeem our sins. So if you do not believe in Jesus Christ at the moment of your death, your soul may not enter the kingdom of heaven.

Buddhists rely on the law of karma to determine the cycle of reincarnation. As a result, if you live in a manner that causes pain and suffering to others, you will build up a big karmic debt and be reborn into poor conditions in the next life as an animal or a human being depending on the severity of your karmic debt.

---

[2] https://www.biography.com/military-figure/joan-of-arc.
[3] https://www.biography.com/scholar/galileo.

The justice system of the world is not always fair or impartial. The fate of humanity is in the hands of the big three—capitalists, politicians, and scientists. With money, power, and technology, they dominate the world and dictate policies that affect nations, communities, and individuals. Laws and regulations are designed to protect the interests of these capitalists, politicians, and scientists. Tax laws can be modified to favor capitalists, powerful politicians can cover up their scandals and corruption, and scientists can persuade the government to fund their projects. In recent years, we have seen several incidents that made us think more deeply about political and social influences on the justice system.

Many problems are clearly visible to those living in the twenty-first century. With science and technology, humans can almost play the role of God with the DNA map to conduct cloning experiments or genetic engineering projects. We continue to develop weapons of mass destruction to kill each other. Our planet is facing the greatest threat in its history. The environment is contaminated due to human abuse and exploitation. The people of the world are living with a false sense of peace and security because the global fear of economic or political instability is suppressed.

Since September 11, 2001, the world has witnessed the ability of fanatics and extremist terrorists who have done heavy damage to many nations. Many terrorist groups may already have nuclear, chemical, and biological weapons that can cause global destruction. They are waiting only for the right moment to strike. Globally, we see catastrophes such as droughts, floods, hurricanes, tidal waves, and tornadoes caused by disturbances of the earth's atmosphere. Many people suffer from famine, disease, poverty, and war.

Humanity has endured many storms from the dawn of time until now. We have gone through deadly plagues, holy wars, world wars, and many other challenges particularly in the past two thousand years. Now we have arrived at a very dangerous intersection between science and spirituality. Because of developments in science and technology, we face total annihilation by numerous methods. We are constantly threatened by reports ranging from weapons of mass destruction in biological, chemical, and nuclear wars to environmental pollution and food contamination. Humankind has the capability to destroy the entire planet stemming from its aggression, egocentricity, greed, hatred, and struggles. Indeed, it may be a very turbulent ordeal the likes of which humanity has never seen before and perhaps will never see again.

Combining information from our daily news with clues from the scriptures or messengers, we can think we are going through a transitional phase. The apostle John reported visions of a war in heaven between the forces of good and evil. From his testimony, Satan and his gang lost the battle in heaven and were thrown down to earth. As a result, the final conflict does not take place in heaven, which is the invisible world. Instead, it will occur in our physical world. Satan and his troops represent the forces of evil and darkness. God also sends many servants to represent the power of faith and truth.

We can use the energetic approach to visualize Satan and his schemes as the lower, negative energy frequencies that fall within the range of power and selfishness. Anyone who is hungry for power or is living in a selfish way has many openings—ambition, envy, greed, and lust for instance—that can attract Satan's attention. The spiritual war occurs first in our heads; they are Satan's battleground as he relentlessly attacks us with disturbing thoughts, emotional swings, frightening visions, enticing temptations, and more. Christians are reminded to put on the armor of God (Ephesians 6:10–17), which means they need to raise their level of consciousness to recognize and overcome Satan's attacks. Satan has a very effective and powerful strategy to tempt people.

Satan is the invisible leader of this world's systems. He controls and influences every aspect of life, e.g., the economy, education, family, politics, religion, and society. He cleverly works through the systems of our cultures, governments, and societies to challenge, distract, and tempt us. God created Satan (negative energy) as a vehicle to measure our will and determination. In prayer, we need vigilance, faith, and perseverance. When we ask God for something in prayer and there is no answer, we need to determine how badly we need it and how determined we are to attain it. Satan will constantly challenge us and even attack us when our prayers are not answered. The challenge is to maintain our focus and our faith.

Perhaps God allows Satan to rule the world in order for Satan to complete his reign and therefore end all evil acts and sin. During Satan's reign, the world's view of good and evil can be challenging. We can see many righteous people being judged and condemned while the villains get away with literal murder. As poor and innocent people, we are just like sheep. We must follow laws that are written by scoundrels in governments, schools, and religions. These crooked politicians, capitalists, and scientists use their money and power to make or change laws to serve their interests. Maybe in God's grand and clever scheme, all souls are given the chance to learn and evolve.

For good and obedient souls to become witnesses of the Light, this darkness can be their true test. God shows love for evil and rebellious souls through the opportunities they are given as they strive to reach their ultimate goal, which is to rule the world. Parents can understand this concept as we raise our children. Many of us have dealt with disobedient and rebellious children. One reason children defy us is because they do not get what they want even if it is not good for them such as too much candy.

On this journey, your nemesis is your best friend. You will learn from each other because your nemesis will constantly challenge you and keep you on your toes helping you to evolve. God created Satan to attack, deceive, and test all His creation. It seems that Satan is becoming more cunning, daring, destructive, and powerful to the point of openly challenging and defying God.

Sometimes, parents' children defy them, and often, the parents acted in a similar fashion when they were young. In this case, God already knows how Satan will act because he is one of His children. God allows Satan to challenge and defy Him and to be powerful and reckless because it is part of Satan's growth.

It also helps all God's children to learn through the tests and examples of the eldest child. You can imagine how strong your soul will be after you have endured the cunning attacks, destructive threats, devious traps, overwhelming powers, and painful torments Satan will throw at you. At that point, you will know you are in fact, the real gold having successfully passed through the intense fire. When you reach that point, you will look back and have a deep respect for those who pushed and trained you. It is the same for some who have gone through military training. When they complete boot camp, they thank the mean and tough drill sergeants who pushed them to their limits.

There are several ways of looking at everything since we have to reexamine our personal failures and problems to learn from them. We can view our personal failures and problems similar to a computer's self-check or update processes. When we function within and interact with the environment and see areas of failure or problems, that indicates that we need to go through a self-check or update procedure to improve ourselves. Approaching it from another angle, we can react to it as we would to a roadblock or detour sign along the freeway. Sometimes when we attempt to do something, we run into a dead end or encounter a big problem that forces us to reconsider our options. At that point, we need to pay attention to the signs.

Perhaps the roadblock sign is there to prevent a danger that lies ahead, or maybe the detour sign can help us to find a safer and better road. We can consider the failure or problem as a test of our strength and resourcefulness. We need all our abilities to stay afloat in the tough and perilous river of life because we will constantly be faced with adversity and challenges! Perhaps we can use the Vietnamese saying *Cái khó ló cái khôn*, "Adversity brings wisdom," as a life vest to help us navigate the stormy oceans of trials and suffering.

Every year, Christians celebrate the resurrection of Jesus Christ. Easter is the culmination of the passion of Christ preceded by Lent, a forty-day period of fasting, prayer, and penance. The last week of Lent is called Holy Week; it contains the three days that commemorate the Last Supper and the preceding foot washing as well as Good Friday. It recalls the crucifixion, death, burial, and resurrection of Jesus. This is a tradition that has been maintained and passed on from the first disciples more than two thousand years ago to today.

When Jesus was arrested and crucified, His disciples went into hiding. They were frightened and disoriented because their Master was supposed to be the Messiah. The disciples of Jesus were hunted down as criminals and persecuted by the Jews and the Romans. During this, the darkest and most critical moment, the disciples were desperate and lost. It seemed that they were holding onto a hopeless belief, and it was precisely at that crucial time that the disciples saw the risen Christ. They saw and touched their resurrected Master and knew what they were experiencing was true. This experience was so real and powerful that it made a major impact on their lives. Subsequently, the disciples devoted their lives to proclaiming His resurrection as truth and even sacrificing themselves to defend the proclamation. The determination, sacrifice, and testimonies of the first disciples succeeded in laying down a very strong foundation.

Jesus's disciples' testimonies and His teachings have lasted for over two thousand years and continue to expand despite trials and persecution; adversity can be a faith builder. Oppression and persecution throughout the history of Christianity made it fertile ground for seeds of faith to grow very strong and deep roots that have helped it survive for more than twenty centuries.

Though the disciples were persecuted, their spirituality was stronger than all the challenging tests in the physical world. They were able to plant seeds of faith in human hearts and souls that have lasted until today. In the twenty-first century, we are generally not hunted down and persecuted, but we are faced with many complex problems revolving around tradition, culture, family, society, religion, economics, politics, and science. Overcoming these challenging tests requires a wise integration of science and spirituality. More important, we have to realize that the spiritual will override the material. If we rely on the material to find the solution, it will be a very limited and transitory solution. Spirituality on the other hand has an infinite range

We can have confidence and brains, but in certain situations, we may not have total clarity, and we can still make mistakes due to the influence of alcohol or drugs, peer pressure, autosuggestion, or mass hysteria that causes us to react in a particular way. It might also be a spiritual influence by which we hear a convincing and overpowering voice that may take control over our minds and bodies. Regardless of the cause, as a result, we can make mistakes, and the damage is done. As we realize this point, we become aware that it depends on each person's ability to handle situations in a positive rather than a negative way. The critical point here is to recognize the mistakes and turn them into good examples and lessons to help others instead of blaming, condemning, or judging others. Instead of creating additional negative vibrations, we can calmly and wisely use these incidents as lessons or examples to help others to understand and thereby prevent them from making the same mistakes. This level of perception requires the capacity of the true self, which can help us to override or control the ego.

By accepting our failures and defeats, we can make them more tolerable and less damaging. When we accept them, it means that we realize we have failed or were defeated. In this mindset, we are not in the state of shock, denial, or bitterness, so we are open to observe the reason we failed or how we were defeated and learn from that; we can be resilient in the face of adversity.

## Chapter 8
# MY COOKING STORY

I am not good in the kitchen because throughout my childhood, my mother did everything, and she did not teach me how to cook. During my college years, I picked up cooking from my friends, and I could make noodles for myself. My wife showed me how to cook, and I can prepare simple meals for the children whenever she is working.

At first, I thought cooking involved formulas and processes, so I approached cooking as a mechanical concept. Sometimes, I was frustrated because of my clumsiness; it took me too long to do simple tasks such as peeling and slicing tomatoes. Due to my clumsiness and lack of experience in the kitchen, I made simple meals, so I had a limited repertoire. Our children enjoyed the variety of dishes my wife could make much more than they enjoyed mine. And when I would leave messes in the kitchen, that would stress out my wife, and there I was cooking to try to reduce stress on her. Over the years, I have improved my cooking skills. I am still far from my wife's level, but I continue to observe and learn.

I was very intimidated the first time I attempted to prepare a meal, but I learned and made adjustments. I could actually see the plate and taste the food to measure my progress. This cooking story reminds me of how I can observe the immediate effects of the neuron firing's adjustments and executions. Since I care and want to make a good meal, I focus my energy and mind on preparing one for my family. It is the same way a mother expresses her love as she prepares the meal for her children.

*Chapter 9*
# MY GRASS CUTTING STORY

I have always thought that mowing the lawn was a simple task. I considered it a cosmetic job since the yard needed to look decent. However, I did not do a good job even though the grass did end up cut. I did not pay much attention to trimming or cleaning up the sidewalk. Eventually, I learned that cutting grass was not as simple as I used to think. It can be an art that someone may enjoy doing, but that was not my case.

I have learned that there are tasks we have to tackle whether we like them or not, and cutting grass is one of mine; it was a way for me to get a workout and show my neighbors that I respected them, so I approached it with a pleasant mindset. By recognizing how everything is interconnected, I realize that I need to add my piece to the puzzle.

I learned that I could turn a normal event into a negative event by allowing my ego and selfishness to affect my approach and attitude. By doing so, I can cause delays, distractions, interruptions, and problems even with simple tasks. So I cut grass with an enthusiastic attitude and accomplish the task with as little friction as possible.

*Chapter 10*
# MY LAUNDRY STORY

Years ago when my boys were younger, I was handling the laundry one day. My wife asked if I had rinsed the boys' underwear before putting them in the washing machine. I had not. She explained that I should because sometimes they were soiled. If I just threw everything in the washing machine at once, the dirty stuff would move to the other clothes.

One day, I did the laundry and told my teenage boys to put away their clean clothes, but they did not because they got distracted. When my wife came home from a long day at work and saw the stacks of clothes in the boys' room, she put them away herself and told me, "If you take on a job, make sure it's completed!" My wife made a valid point when she said that all the incomplete or mishandled tasks would eventually come back to her.

I remember these incidents because they are good reminders for me to complete jobs I take on even though I encounter difficulties, obstacles, or problems. As I follow through, I realize that adversity brings wisdom and develops resiliency.

PART IV

## Chapter 11
# VITAMINS FROM THE FRUITS OF MISFORTUNE

By knowing or seeing the mistakes other people made, we learn or adapt or change the way we think, say, and act to avoid making the same ones. This is the ideal way. But if we do not know or cannot change, we will eventually make the same mistakes and go through a similar learning curve. In the end, we will gain the knowledge from those difficult lessons.

On my way to work one night, I was in the right lane on a three-lane road. After the light turned green, we proceeded, and the car in front of me wanted to get into the left lane to make a left turn at an upcoming traffic light. I slowed down so the driver could make his move, but a driver behind me honked in frustration and expressed his frustration when he passed the car in front of me. I heard a voice saying, *It could have been worse if one of those drivers had had a gun—road rage.* Anger can explode and lead to violence.

We need to be more patient and tolerant. We all at one point or another have been lost in a new city and caused little traffic jams. We wished the other drivers would show a little more patience and understanding. But we can become jumpy or frustrated when somebody cuts in front of us. We can diffuse the whole situation when we place ourselves in the other driver's seat and reminded ourselves that we were once the annoying driver who asked the other drivers for patience and tolerance. This is the way we benefit from the vitamins of failure. Instead of being angry or frustrated, we can be calm and understanding and give our fellow drivers a break, a win-win situation as they can get to their destinations and we are not stressed out.

I just use the example of fruits and vitamins to present the idea of how we can benefit from the bad or negative situations in life. If I am a careless person who continues to cause problems for myself or others in the family and at work, eventually, as I realize the source of my carelessness and learn from those errors, I enhance my knowledge. So in this particular case, from the fruit of carelessness, I get vitamin K—Knowledge. In the same manner, because of envy I hurt my friends and when I actually recognize how it affects my own life, I can change. Through these experiences, I gain something from the fruit of envy and benefit from its vitamin A—Altruism, and vitamin B— Benevolence.

I have felt the agony of defeat many times. In college, I was a fierce competitor in basketball and tennis. When I won a game, I was arrogant, and when I lost, I was angry and dejected. But as I grew older, I saw another side of the fruit of defeat and found vitamin H—Humility. If a greedy person fails and loses everything and desperately seeks help from others, he or she discovers the meaning of altruism. This person tasted the fruit of greed and got its vitamin A—Altruism.

I came up with this table of vitamins and their fruits.

| Fruits | Vitamins |
|--------|----------|
| Carelessness | K (Knowledge) |
| Defeat | H (Humility) |
| Envy | A (Altruism), B (Benevolence) |
| Greed | A (Altruism) |
| Isolation | D (Determination) |
| Hatred | A (Altruism), B (Benevolence) |
| Lost | D (Determination) |
| Oppression | C (Courage) |
| Pain | E (Empathy) |
| Selfishness | A (Altruism), K (Knowledge) |
| Sin | E (Empathy), H (Humility) |
| Violence | B (Benevolence), H (Humility) |

We all need to be ready for unexpected changes, difficult challenges, and disastrous failures. We prepare ourselves physically, mentally, and spiritually by being observant and conscious. We apply the energetic approach to monitor and adapt ourselves to the changes in the surrounding energy field. Our bodies become dynamic systems that are always updating and changing themselves with the environment, the global network of energy fields and data.

We can remind ourselves not to become too comfortable with the feelings of winning or success because they will invariably cause us to fall headlong into an idle, inflexible, and lazy condition. We should apply the techniques of the heaven-earth-human elements when we are riding the high tide of success and learn from these lessons so we can handle ourselves when we hit the low tide of loss or failure. We should not set our expectations too high because that will bring illusions and stress to us. It is better that we plan and hope for the best but expect or prepare for the worst. Since we are always prepared for the unexpected or worst case, we have a level of adaptability and flexibility.

In February and early March 2020, we faced the COVID-19 pandemic and everything changed. The coronavirus has shifted the thinking process as well as the living standards of the entire human race. Now, we have included the options of self-quarantine, social distancing, virtual meetings, and wearing face masks. There will be new paradigms, and the principles of energy and life will become the new standards.

At important transitions in human history, the Creator sent capable souls to set the standards and raise the bar. For example, at the end of the nineteenth century, God sent Marie Curie (1867–1934), Thomas Edison (1847–1931), Albert Einstein (1879–1955), Henry Ford (1864–1947), Wilbur Wright (1867–1912), and Orville Wright (1871–1948) to name a few. These souls have shifted our living conditions from the nineteenth century to the modern world of today with aircraft, cars, radios, telephones, etc. In 2021, our world and way of life have changed due to the pandemic, economic problems, natural disasters, social injustice, and violence.

God just needs one of His smallest agents, a virus, to stop the whole world. Our economic, political, social, and technological systems run like engines with many connected parts. We think we are in control and believe we have all the answers. When we become too arrogant and ignorant, God needs only one tiny virus to completely shut down the engine. We are so distracted with our daily routines and mundane concerns that most of us neglect or deny God. It took only a tiny virus to send a strong message all over the world, "Wash your hands!" It is a simple message, but we neglected it due to distractions, ignorance, and laziness; now, this virus lets everybody around the world hear it.

We need a new way of looking at how we coexist with our natural living environment. Since the Industrial Revolution, we have been exploiting and destroying our planet. We also declared war on the living organisms in the microscopic environment around us. We intend to exterminate or weaponize bacteria, microbes, and viruses instead of finding ways to coexist with them. By doing so, we actually weaken our immune systems because we use chemicals to fight the bacteria or viruses rather than build up our natural defense mechanisms. We rely on antibacterial products more than on our natural immune system. Thousands of years ago, our ancestors did not have antibacterial soap or disinfecting wipes, but they adapted well with nature. They understood the balance and lived in harmony with Mother Nature. There was a mutual respect between humans and all living creatures. Now, we abuse Mother Nature and kill all living creatures because of our selfishness and power struggles. The coronavirus is only one of many microorganisms on earth, but it is strong enough to affect all humans and change the way we live.

We are sharing Earth with other living creatures and especially microorganisms that had been here from the beginning. These microorganisms were on our planet billions of years ago while the human species was here about 500,000 years ago; we are the newcomers. These microorganisms have gone through billions of years to adapt to the changes of our home planet. As human beings, we think we are the superior species, and we take over the entire planet. Driven by greed, power, and selfishness, we are depleting our natural resources and causing mass extinctions. Consequently, our planet is reacting to these drastic changes we have made to heal itself and to preserve all its creatures.

Now, we are in another transition to a new level of the twenty-first century that humans are supposed to have more abilities as foreseen by many visionaries. Our heavenly Father wants all humans to be one with Him and to live in harmony with the world He created for us. We have gone too far off track because of greed, selfishness, and the hunger for power. We are actually on the path of self-destruction, and the coronavirus is a warning sign just like the LED letting us know our car's engine is overheating and will break down if we ignore it.

We are very fortunate to be on earth during this historic time, and more important, we are blessed to be a part of God's plan for the transition from twentieth-century chaos to a twenty-first-century level of global consciousness. Our great-grandchildren will read about us and our time. This is the only chance we can actually contribute what is in our hearts and minds to the global consciousness to help humanity. For that reason, the fire is burning in my heart and soul, and I try my best to share my vision with you. Together, we will make it work, and by doing so, this process will be duplicated and we will see the number of participants increase exponentially.

We are in a difficult and turbulent time with the pandemic, social unrest, natural disasters, terrorism, and violence. I wish to share two stories from the Vietnam War to remind us of the essence of resiliency.

## Chapter 12
# THE BOAT PEOPLE STORY

After the fall of Saigon in 1975, the world began to learn about the Vietnamese boat people, thousands of refugees who fled the invading Communists and took their chances by sailing out into the Pacific. There were many remarkable stories of how they managed to survive under the most difficult conditions and against overwhelming odds.

I knew one of them; we went to college together in the early and mid-1980s. My friend Kevin managed to get on a boat to leave Vietnam without his parents and siblings because they could not go. No one on board realized how dangerous the rough sea would be. When the boat ran out of fuel, these people were lost in the middle of the Pacific Ocean. They also ran out of food and water. Many people began to face the painful truth that they might not survive, and they prayed for a swift death. Miraculously, the boat was rescued by another ship, and these people were given a second chance to live.

My friend came to California and studied to get a bachelor's degree. He was very determined and focused. After graduating, he found a good job and worked hard. Eventually, he saved up enough to sponsor his entire family, and they were united in America. I have always admired his faith and perseverance. I use this story as a reminder of how we should receive God's blessings, grace, and love. If we really recognize it and gratefully conduct ourselves, His blessings and love will flourish. On the contrary, if we blindly or ignorantly waste the opportunities God gives us and live in a destructive or selfish manner, the blessings will disappear.

When I was in California during the 1980s and 1990s, I often heard or read many sad stories about Vietnamese refugees who were arrested or killed because of their destructive or reckless lifestyles that involved addictions, drinking, gambling, crime, and violence. If we are in this darkness, we may be struggling or sinking deeper because of the turbulent waves of ripple effects we created. However, when we reach the point of total desperation and truly ask for God's mercy, He will help us just as He has helped many of His children who were lost or hopeless throughout history.

# Chapter 13
# A CHRISTMAS MESSAGE

On Tuesday, December 24, 2019, I went to bed in the morning after returning home from the overnight shift. I was tired and fell into a deep sleep. I had a vivid and wonderful dream that I wrote down when I woke up. In the dream, I was floating in an empty space, a dark void. Then came the Word … it was like the first thought of creation, and everything was created. At that point, I was given an explanation to understand the Word as the cosmic design specification or the data structure of the universe. It would be similar to the DNA as the genetic code for all living creatures; the Word contains the design specifications of the universe as well as its components including dimensions, galaxies, planets, and species.

I was led to see the cosmic timeline in order to have a view of the design specifications. On the timeline, the cosmic clock started at T=0 and the Word appeared from nothing, the void. I can refer to this point as the first thought of creation. I can relate to the command "Let there be light" (Genesis 1:3), in which we had the distinction between the light, day, and the dark, night. I view it as a command or data structure that defines the formation of the cosmic system—photons, electrons, protons, matter, and antimatter.

Next, I found myself at T ≈ 4 BC to witness the transformation of the Word into a physical body (John 1:14). I still remember the angel's proclamation of the Christ's birth in Vietnamese, *Vinh danh Thiên Chúa trên trời, bình an dưới thế cho người thiện tâm*, "Glory to God in the highest, and on earth peace among those with whom he is pleased!" (Luke 2:14 ESV). I went to a French Catholic school in Vietnam, and we heard or repeated this passage many times as we celebrated Christmas. Additionally, I was reminded of this passage.

> He is the image of the invisible God, the firstborn of all creation. For by him all things were created, in heaven and on earth, visible and invisible, whether thrones or dominions or rulers or authorities—all things were created through him and for him. And he is before all things, and in him all things hold together. (Colossians 1:15–17 ESV)

I could interpret it as the transformation from God to human, or from the Word in $n$-D ($n$-dimension where $n = \infty$) to a 3-D format on Earth. Jesus was the embodiment of the Word, the living encyclopedia of the cosmic design specification. He tried to teach the disciples by using parables, but they could not understand and continued to ask Him to elaborate. He tried to teach and show us how to connect to the source to find our way home and to navigate the lost world.

I was given a vision of the Lord's Supper when Jesus told the disciples to continue to perform this communion in His memory. I interpret this as the way He gave us apps or software to download so we can get the direct connection to the Word or cosmic design specification. Jesus is described as the Advocate, Comforter, Helper, and Holy Spirit.

Nowadays, we are bombarded with millions of apps that seems to be exciting, important, and profitable, but many of us have totally ignored or in some cases completely deleted the most important apps or software. By looking at the conditions of our world, we can see the consequences of this. People are distracted, lost, and trapped because of abuse, deception, greed, hatred, power, and selfishness.

We desperately need to remind each other that on this historic day, our Creator decided to come into our world to share His love and wisdom with us. A loving Father, who ruled the universe, decided to step into our little play house to be among His children. Naturally, when He was inside our play house, He had to play along and follow the role play here. Many parents become childlike themselves to play with and share joy with their children. It is an act of love as we leave our mature or adult selves outside and adapt to the children's playbook to experience their imaginary worlds. Now I could have a clearer understanding of how Jesus really tried to follow our human playbook, and along the way, He wanted to use those scenarios to teach or help us. But we were too distracted by the material world or our playbook and totally missed His message.

# Chapter 14
# A GRATEFUL PRAYER

On Tuesday, August 24, 2020, when I was asleep, I was overwhelmed by the grace our heavenly Parents have given us. I woke up and expressed my thoughts in the form of a prayer. I hope you can find this grace especially if you are facing difficult trials in the dark storm. This is my grateful prayer.

My heavenly Father, the omnipotent!
My holy Mother, the merciful!
My Lord Master, the divine!
I place my heart and soul before You to humbly and respectfully express my gratitude for the love You have given me. I have often asked, "Why me?" I know I really do not deserve Your blessings. Despite all my failings and mistakes, You continue to overwhelm me with the divine grace and unconditional love that I cannot fully fathom. My soul is arrogant, sinful, and weak. You did not judge or condemn; instead, You saved me and gave me the chance to live with a purpose.

You covered me with grace even though I was disobedient. You embraced me with love even though I showed resentment, disrespect, and hatred toward You. You opened the door to give me many opportunities to help others even though I was blind and ignorant. You are the wise Father, the benevolent Mother, and the divine Master. I light this candle of faith in my heart as a sign of my deep gratitude. I devote my mind to use this tiny candle of faith to ignite the flame of Your love and radiate the warmth of Your grace to everybody around me.

I say this prayer with the open heart and mind, truthfulness, and humility as a little voice in the middle of an overwhelming and turbulent storm that affects the whole world. I know You heard my prayers and responded in many ways to give me comfort, encouragement, faith, and strength at the exact moments I desperately needed that. I am just one of Your children, and my prayer is a reflection of how much You care for and love all living creatures. Many people are drowning or struggling in this dark storm, and they desperately need Your guidance and support. I send my prayer of gratitude as a beacon of hope for others to recognize that You are ready to help anyone who asks with an open heart and mind, truthfulness, and humility.

I always find comfort and wisdom in Your words. As I was capturing these thoughts to express my prayer, I saw this message and included it here as a profound reminder for myself and others: "Great peace have those who love your law; nothing can make them stumble" (Psalm 119:165 ESV).

You have transformed a disobedient, hateful, ignorant, sinful, and weak soul into an effective witness of Your grace and love. The best way I can show my gratitude is to pass on this knowledge and help people find Your presence, amen.

## Chapter 15
# SEVEN LAYERS OF THE RAINBOW

One day when I was meditating, I saw an image that could be used either as a book cover or a presentation. The art of resiliency is the process by which we develop as we are planted on earth and nurtured by fertilizers such as anger, doubt, fear, injustice, power, and selfishness. Eventually, we harvest the golden opportunities to reach the seven layers of the rainbow—abundance, happiness, peace, health, success, unity, and enlightenment. When we can nurture the food of misfortune and produce golden opportunities, we will gradually see the seven layers of the rainbow. Here is the description of the seven layers.

**Abundance** is the first layer. We recover and reach a state of equilibrium in which we have abundance. This is not driven by ambition, greed, or selfishness. The abundant energy provides for the benefits and needs of the whole, not the individual. Money is a form of energy. Depending on how I spend money, I can generate negative or positive ripples in my home, family, and community.

**Happiness** is the second layer. We achieve it when we stabilize our lives because we have abundant resources to achieve personal goals and help others.

**Peace** is the third layer. We will experience radiant serenity after we have abundance and happiness.

**Health** is the fourth layer. It is clear that health will follow the first three layers. When we have enough of everything, we are happy and peaceful. As a result, we will be healthy mentally and physically.

**Success** is the fifth layer. I am not referring here to success in terms of academics, careers, finances, or relationships; I am talking about being successful in realizing our lives' purposes and achieving them.

**Unity** is the sixth layer. At this point, we become the bridge between the physical and spiritual realms.

**Enlightenment** is the seventh layer. We will reach the ultimate level of understanding and understand how all things are interconnected. We are all connected to the cosmic network system to recognize the depth of universal wisdom.

Based on this view, one of the first steps we can take to develop the art of resiliency is to open our hearts and minds to God's presence in us. One of our effective tools in life is the opening of our intuitive potential because that will enable us to discover God's presence in and around us. To activate our intuitive potential, we need openness, truthfulness, and humility. (I will discuss more about opening our intuitive potential later.)

This is the first step, and not everyone can meet all three conditions mentioned above and have the opening of their intuitive potential. Due to the challenging and turbulent conditions of the world, people are anxious, busy, sick, suffering, and unhappy, and it is not easy to meet all three conditions. Some of them are lucky just to meet one or two. For example, it is not easy for people to keep open hearts and minds and be truthful when they are unjustly abused; it is a challenge for people to be humble when they have fame, money, and power; it is very difficult for people who are aggressive and unscrupulous to be truthful and humble.

Some people are enduring such pain and suffering that they are fortunate to be open, truthful, and humble. Others are desperate, lost, and weak, and it would be a challenge for them to be open, truthful, and humble. Some battle distractions, doubts, and fears, and it is not easy for them to be open, truthful, and humble much less grateful. I found it difficult to be open, truthful, and humble when my life was completely destroyed in that fatal car accident. I was arrogant and confident that I was in control of my fate and destiny, but God showed up and taught me a lesson. I was not grateful in the beginning for that. In fact, I was hurt and resentful. However, being a graceful and loving parent, God patiently allowed me to vent my rage and despair. Then I was able to open my heart and mind to recognize His grace and love, be truthful about my failures and limited knowledge, and be humble in His presence.

I had been blinded by my selfish ambition, but God helped me open my heart and mind. I was deceived by my ego, but God let me see my soul, my true self, through this near-death experience. I was doing so well in California that I believed nobody could change my destiny, but God crushed my ego in less than a second, and I learned to be humble in His presence. It took many years for me to overcome the painful suffering and gradually be thankful. But the first step was to be open, truthful, and humble to allow God to enter my heart and mind.

Over the years, it became my daily routine to pray and express my gratitude whether I had had a peaceful or a stormy day. It takes an experienced or mature soul to focus on God's grace and be thankful because we live in a very chaotic, difficult, and toxic world. It is not easy for people to understand the reasons things happen especially when they face calamity, injustice, and violence.

Children can resent their parents' disciplining them, but when they mature, they realize the importance of being reprimanded and actually thank their parents for the discipline they gave them. They will be more grateful when they become parents and have to raise their own children.

We should be grateful for the difficult or tough lessons! It takes a mature or experienced soul to know this because most people will be angry and doubtful and turn from God when they face painful or unjust trials. I was one of these souls who actually screamed at God, "Why are you doing this to me? You're not fair!"

As God reveals Himself more and allows me to understand Him better, I feel very grateful because if God really reaches out to help and guide a lowly, sinful, and weak soul like myself, for sure He will not abandon anyone. I know many of your souls are more experienced and mature than mine because God had to use extreme measures to awaken me. To correct me, God had to sacrifice three persons—my fiancée and two drunk men. If God took that much effort to save my arrogant, disobedient, sinful, and weak soul, He will do the same or more to help you. If there is a reason to be grateful, this is it. God really revealed Himself to me as He embraced me tightly even as I was venting. When I was totally at peace and felt the grace and love He gave me, my only question was, "Why me?" Out of seven billion souls in this chaotic world, I was sure there were many souls who were more deserving and needy than my arrogant and lowly soul.

Now I know the reason; it was not my soul that God was saving. He used this insignificant soul to reach out to those who were trapped in darkness. God guided me through a journey that began when I was in total darkness after my car crash. Over the years, He allowed me to see the various layers of His blessings, and now, I refer to the symbolic seven-layer rainbow. I believe if you find and trust God as you go through the dark and difficult times, He will guide and help you see this seven-layer rainbow.

# PART V

## Chapter 16
# FIND A MEANING OR PURPOSE

I had many conversations with my coworker, John, and one day, we touched on the subject of human suffering. I continued to meditate on it and suddenly saw the scale of human suffering. On this scale, I could see the ranges from 1 to 10, 10 being the worst. I consider the experiences of the people in the Nazi death camps to be a 10 because of the atrocity and evil they had to face. Dr. Viktor Frankl, a death camp survivor, described in his book *Man's Search for Meaning* that many inmates had no hope and were living corpses waiting to be sent to the gas chamber. The Holocaust is the most ruthless event in history, and it sends a strong reminder to future generations to never make the same mistake again.

Holocaust survivors had a level of fear, hopelessness, isolation, and pain that humankind had never experienced before. People recognized Frankl's purpose as he shared his experiences from the darkest depth of human suffering. This is a statement about Frankl's purpose in life, "The meaning of your life is to help others find the meaning of theirs" (Frankl, 165).

There is a wide range to human suffering. Someone who loses a job could consider that a 10 on my human suffering scale, but losing a job might be just a 1 for someone fighting cancer. When we are in the midst of a difficult trial, we often think our situation is the worst because we do not have a clear purpose or meaning of life. Frankl wrote, "People have enough to live by but nothing to live for; they have the means but no meaning" (Frankl, 140). Frankl spent the rest of his life helping people find their meaning of life through the principle of logotherapy, which is taught at the Viktor Frankl Institute (www.viktorfrankl.org). He wrote, "In some ways suffering ceases to be suffering at the moment it finds a meaning, such as the meaning of a sacrifice" (Frankl, 113).

I found an approach that helped me find my meaning or purpose when I was suffering in the darkness. When I was totally helpless and hopeless, I suddenly heard the encouraging voice from my inner self. It was the guidance from this soft, inner voice that became my compass and GPS (global positioning system).

Many people finding themselves conflicted have tried to find different ways to receive a clear vision and understanding when choosing between the material and spiritual paths. After taking so many wrong turns or falling into many holes, we realize that our human view is shortsighted. Using the modern example of the GPS, we can say our device has many flaws and cannot accurately give a long-range scan because it is easily disrupted by surrounding interference, so we look for a better guidance system. Throughout history, many people were gifted with the ability to have a communication link with the higher beings. Some examples include Joan of Arc, who was instructed to help France; Francis of Assisi as he received the calling to repair the church; Catherine of Siena, who wrote *The Dialogue*; and Bernadette Soubirous, who saw the Virgin Mary. They had obtained knowledge that ordinary people would never have been able to attain let alone understand because of their weak minds and unchanging hearts. Furthermore, we live in a world that is ruled by power and selfishness. These energy frequencies and interfering signals can overshadow the beam of the guidance system especially when they pose a threat or present a conflict of interest.

We can connect to and seek guidance from the higher beings. Consider the help menus on our computers that offer us the proper guidance to operate the computer. Compare this to cosmic knowledge, the universal operating system. When we face difficult problems or dangers, we can invoke this help key for guidance and avoid making errors. Particularly since 1917, we have had many reported incidents of the Virgin Mary appearing around the world. Mary was sending the warning messages and asking humanity to change or face the dire consequences of our greedy, power driven, and selfish actions.

These messengers were absolutely convinced that the voices they heard came from above or beyond the physical realm. Many of them tried to explain that these voices were very clear just as if they were listening to someone speaking next to them. They also identified that the voices came from many different sources such as God, Jesus, Mary, angels, and saints.

Information can be encoded, transmitted, and executed in a computer system. We can break it down into three components: syntax, semantics, and pragmatics. Generally speaking, syntax is the format of a message, semantics is the meaning of a message, and pragmatics is the purpose of the communication. Information is a sequence of data that record or transmit a message. It can be recorded as signs or conveyed as signals by waves. In a computer system, the basic unit of information is a bit, a binary digit—0 or 1. On a larger scale, however, information can be described as a type of input to an organism or system. Some inputs are important to the functions of the organism, for example, food. Others are important to the systems themselves; energy is an example of this.

Information is any type of pattern that influences the formation or transformation of other patterns. If information has been perceived by a conscious mind, the specific context associated with this interpretation may cause the transformation of the information into knowledge. For example, when we practice meditation, we may receive data information either as voices (sonic frequencies) or visions (electrophotonic frequencies).

It is written in the Bible, "In the beginning was the Word, and the Word was with God, and the Word was God" (John 1:1 ESV). In the original Greek translation it was λόγος, logos, the word. In a computer system, *word* is a term for the natural unit of data used by a particular processor design. If we can receive the Word, we would be able to adapt to the universal design.

The initial Word was the original, primordial beacon that created the universe. Cosmic energy has an infinite frequency range or a data frame with $n^n$ combinations (where $n = \infty$). For example, the 8-bit data frame would have $2^8$ or 256 combinations. Consequently, with our limitations in the three-dimensional world, how can we capture the full content of the Word? It is impossible to use physical or electronic devices to calibrate the entire spectrum of cosmic energy, but we can use the human brain to receive or transmit the combined frequencies of cosmic energy. Just like in mathematics, we cannot get the exact value of pi ($\pi$) because it is an irrational and transcendental number, but we can express it as pi = circumference ÷ diameter. A beacon started the original transmission from the first moment when the primeval atom was created. This radio signal still exists. Radio astronomers can detect this signal, and they have named it cosmic microwave background radiation.

A weather station transmits a periodic, continuous signal on a specified radio frequency to provide meteorological information. The Earth transmits its signal to provide us a variety of information such as geological, seismic, gravitational, and electromagnetic data. The physical body transmits vital signs such as blood pressure, heart rate, temperature, and respiratory rate. If we can attune our senses to catch the beacons transmitted by our body, our planet, and the universe, we may be able to change or adjust our lifestyles to be in sync with these energy fields.

The beacon signal gets stronger (higher intensity) or the energy vibration increases as we approach a certain event or timing getting closer to the red zone. This beacon signal detector was preinstalled in the brain as a part of our evolution, and sometimes, we rely on this intuition more than on our logical processes. To fully develop this capacity, we need to have a key similar to the software activation key to start using it.

In March 2020, I was finalizing this book when the coronavirus pandemic hit. I watched the daily news to follow the condition of this pandemic, and one night, I was reminded of the similar concern when I watched the news daily to find out about the Communists getting closer to Saigon as one city after another continued to fall during April 1975. When they entered Saigon, it would be game over, and we could not stop them. Fortunately, this time, we have the resources and cooperation from all countries to slow the spread of and eventually treat the coronavirus.

The human body is a highly advanced biocomputer system. In this design, the biocomputer has an operating system that constantly monitors all the functions and maintains the integrity of its data structure. I use the example of the operating system to describe the role of our conscience or true self. Additionally, our Creator has many I/O devices to communicate with His subjects. It was written, "The hearing ear and the seeing eye, the Lord has made them both" (Proverbs 20:12 ESV). He can utilize various means such as animals, humans, living organisms, or nature. For example, God can use a dog to communicate and help somebody to cope with the loss of a loved one, or He can use a bacteria to warn us to be more conscious of what we eat.

Our Creator designed a highly sophisticated GPS that is unique for each person. I have learned to listen to and trust God's advice. This is my reminder especially when I find myself in the midst of turbulent storm or lost in the darkness: "And now, O sons, listen to me: blessed are those who keep my ways. Hear instruction and be wise, and do not neglect it" (Proverbs 8:32–33 ESV).

At one time or another, we have wanted to do something but heard a voice telling us not to do it. Due to the fact that we were distracted, inexperienced, or impulsive, we ignored the warning. As a result, we ran into problems or faced strong opposition and could not reach our objective. We usually said afterward, "I should have listened to my inner voice" or "I should have followed my intuition." Depending on our level of consciousness, the next time, we may not remember because we are still overwhelmed by all the circumstances and ignore the soft or silent warning as we fall again. But in some cases, we remember and pay attention to our inner voice or intuition to see the positive effects or changes. Gradually, we begin to realize the significant values of the inner voice, or intuition.

To help you remember this important fact, I use the acronym

YODA, Your Old Divine Advisor. Our Creator equipped us with a special communication link; YODA is the true self who had been with our souls from the beginning. Our bodies do not last, but our souls, the essence of our being, continues to exist. It has a large wisdom base as it collects all your experiences over many lifetimes. YODA is the force in you. When you are facing difficult situations, let go of your logical mind or feelings and listen to YODA. On the journey of life, most of us select the manual mode as we attempt to utilize our knowledge and logic to navigate challenging and unknown territories. However, we have all experienced moments when we were totally lost or desperate and had to switch to autopilot and trust the guidance of the GPS. However, as soon as we get back to familiar territory, we switch back to manual mode. After many times of being lost and finding our way with the GPS, we began to trust and use it more often. Many of us go in circles as we rely only on the manual mode to navigate life. When we make the switch from manual mode to autopilot and allow the GPS to guide us, we will discover the purpose of our journey.

# Chapter 17
## THE GOD-PRESENCE ATTRIBUTE

One primary purpose of our lives is to reach the full capacity of the God-presence attribute (GPA) in us. We were made in God's image, and at one point, our ancestors had a high level of GPA because they were living in harmony with nature. But as we made technological advancements, we became dependent on these devices and gradually our GPA level went down drastically; as a result, we lost our faith and purpose. Now, we are easily depressed or hopeless when we encounter trials and problems. It is very important to remind ourselves of the GPA and focus on its development.

We need to develop and raise our GPA level. Some of us operate with GPA levels between 70 and 90 percent. By fate, some of us had many experiences of GPA in life to hold a strong and unwavering faith. With a deep understanding of God's timing and wisdom, we trust Him. God has a tactical plan in mind when He moves each of us to a particular position on His giant chessboard that may be tough to handle. By recognizing the movements or chain of events and understanding the important period or cycle of transitions, we show total obedience to God. When He places us in a pivotal position, we need to have strength, to trust and obey Him, and to stand firm. We will then be able to observe how His plan unfolds around us. This is what many of our ancestors experienced. We have read incredible stories about

- Abraham, who faced the ultimate test of faith as he brought Isaac to the altar,

- Moses, who faced Pharaoh, the most powerful ruler on earth,
- Noah, who faced the biggest natural disaster in history,
- Joseph, who faced the tough trials of injustice, isolation, imprisonment, and slavery, and
- Shadrach, Meshach, and Abednego, who defied King Nebuchadnezzar and faced death in the furnace.

We need this high level of GPA to stand firm without doubt or fear. The world is in a storm because people are bombarded by concerns, distractions, doubts, lies, and speculations about the pandemic; they are overwhelmed by waves of negative energy. During this critical time, God will use those who have unwavering faith and absolute trust in Him as effective and reliable instruments.

We can monitor the GPA level that can be from 0 percent to 100 percent as shown below.

- From 0 to 30 percent: We have no or very little experience of God's presence. We are spiritually immature, ignorant, and weak. We are easily lost and trapped in the darkness of doubt, fear, pain, and suffering.
- From 30 to 50 percent: We have had some experiences of God's presence, but we are still 50/50 in terms of our faith, and our logical mind usually takes over. We are the ordinary and vulnerable human beings who constantly struggle with deception, distraction, and temptation.
- From 50 to 70 percent: We have had good experiences of God's presence and are capable, disciplined, and responsible. We have a level of faith to put our trust in God.
- From 70 to 99 percent: The experience of God's presence is a major part of our lives. We become extraordinary human beings such as the sages, saints, and religious founders in the past. For example, we can imagine that perhaps Abraham or Moses experienced God's presence 90 percent of the time and had direct communication with and guidance from God. They became His mouth, eyes, and ears.

- 100 percent GPA is Jesus Christ.

> In the beginning was the Word, and the Word was
> with God, and the Word was God. He was in the
> beginning with God. All things were made through
> him, and without him was not any thing made that
> was made. In him was life, and the life was the light
> of men. (John 1:1–4 ESV)

Many messengers, prophets, saints, and teachers showed ranges
of God's presence up to 99 percent. Prince Siddhartha pushed himself
to the extreme limit, and perhaps he reached 99 percent when he
became the Enlightened One, the Buddha. But only one human
being reached 100 percent—Jesus Christ. This is the presence of God
incarnate. Jesus said,

> Whoever believes in me will also do the works that I
> do; and greater works than these will he do, because
> I am going to the Father. Whatever you ask in my
> name, this I will do, that the Father may be glorified
> in the Son. (John 14:12–13 ESV)

This is the mark of a true Master who wanted His disciples to
excel and achieve more than He had.

Finding a purpose or meaning will determine the level of control
we have over our lives. In manual mode, we rely on our navigational
instincts and skills to deal with crosswinds, storms, turbulence, and
so forth. But when we are on autopilot, the GPS already knows the
weather, wind direction, and atmosphere, and it guides us.

With a GPA of 0 percent to 30 percent, you rely on your logical
brain 70 percent up to 100 percent. As you progress and improve your
GPA to the range of 50 percent to 70 percent, you let YODA guide you
up to 70 percent. When you reach the GPA of 90 percent, you allow
God to take control of 90 percent and the remaining 10 percent would
be your own decisions on basic human issues such food and shelter.

## Chapter 18
# THE ART OF PEACEMAKING

We are witnessing the dangerous and negative consequences of our hostile, repulsive, selfish, and unforgiving behavior. Everything seems all right for most people because they still have their jobs, homes, and possessions. But as we continue to be ignorant and reckless, we intentionally or unintentionally declare war on Mother Nature and all creatures.

Since we are made in God's image and likeness, we should have a level of responsibility and wisdom to take care of our own species and planet. We really need to be peacemakers on multiple levels—with Mother Nature, all living creatures, and ourselves. We need to be in energetic harmony with Mother Nature, to be consciously responsible for the welfare of all living creatures, and to be wisely respectful of other human beings.

To be effective peacemakers, we need to consider the following.

- We should have open minds and hearts to understand others without condemning or judging them.
- We should attempt to improve our situations. We are truthful to ourselves as we act in a constructive manner for the benefits of others, not because of power struggles or selfish reasons.
- We should be humble. We should focus on people's concerns, priorities, and problems and offer our services and undivided attention. We wisely exercise humility and act when there is a potential win-win solution. We can understand what Jesus

Christ said: "Blessed are the meek, for they shall inherit the earth" (Matthew 5:5 ESV).

The art of peacemaking requires compassion, wisdom, and courage connected to our GPA. Here are several biblical reminders of these points.

> Blessed are the peacemakers, for they shall be called sons of God. (Matthew 5:9 ESV)

> What you have learned and received and heard and seen in me—practice these things, and the God of peace will be with you. (Philippians 4:9 ESV)

> And let the peace of Christ rule in your hearts, to which indeed you were called in one body. And be thankful. (Colossians 3:15 ESV)

Jesus said, "Do not resist the one who is evil. But if anyone slaps you on the right cheek, turn to him the other also" (Matthew 5:39). For more than twenty centuries, not many humans have followed His advice because their minds and hearts were controlled by selfishness and power struggles. We chose to condemn evil and retaliate against acts of abuse, hatred, and violence. Few can follow Jesus's example of remaining silent and forgiving those who insulted and hurt Him: "Father, forgive them, for they know not what they do" (Luke 23:34 ESV).

The GPA has revealed a profound approach to diffuse this toxic and volatile situation when you are the target of somebody's rage. This person may strike or slap you on the cheek for whatever reason. With a high GPA level, you are able to take the blow or absorb the negative energy without any problem. You are able to show restraint, patience, and forgiveness as if a child had hit you. In the same manner, God loves His children and shows them compassion, forgiveness, and understanding even though we offend Him. God knows our nature just as parents know the mindsets of their children and teens.

This principle is very important particularly in the United States because people are allowed to carry concealed firearms. Therefore, you might suffer more than a proverbial slap on the cheek. We should focus on developing our GPA to utilize compassion, wisdom, and courage to handle these potential situations better. Jesus Christ showed the highest degree of compassion, wisdom, and courage when He endured all the accusations, beatings, humiliation, suffering, and torture, and we should emulate His example as best we can. It can be wise to walk away after a person slaps you on the cheek because you know there is no chance of reasoning with that person then. By blindly following the advice of turning the other cheek, you might put yourself at risk of being seriously wounded or even killed. You must utilize your compassion, wisdom, and courage together, not one or two out of the three.

Using our intuitive potential to observe everything from the perspective of energy and information, we can prevent or handle outbursts of negative energy between two people. First, we should look deep into the issue to know the source of this conflict. To really see the source of the conflict or problem, we need to have these three elements.

- With open minds and hearts, we can see beyond the duality of black and white, good and evil, high and low, and right and wrong.
- We should be truthful in the way we observe or analyze information.
- Humility is the best way to approach and understand others.

When we identify the source of the conflict, we should find a way to settle it. Using the three elements mentioned above, we apply the following qualities.

- Compassion will help us cultivate patience, sympathy, and tolerance.
- Wisdom will help us know how to react and handle ourselves as well as the situation.
- Courage will help us develop fortitude, endurance, and resilience.

After we have successfully handled these issues, we should maintain harmony and pass on the knowledge to help others. Through this, we derive the following benefits.

- We have discovered another peaceful way of helping ourselves and others.
- We have experienced the impact of the level of our GPA.
- We have learned how to transform negative or toxic energy into positive and harmonious energy.

## Chapter 19
# THE NAPALM GIRL STORY

One of the most famous images of the Vietnam War is the photo of the napalmed girl. Through this difficult trial, Mrs. Phan Thi Kim Phuc became God's effective instrument of faith and forgiveness. In her book *Fire Road: The Napalm Girl's Journey through the Horrors of War to Faith, Forgiveness, and Peace*, she shared these inspiring thoughts.

> For more than half of those events, I was able to take questions at the end from the audience, and during those Q&A sessions I noticed a trend. People from all over the globe told me time and again that when they first say my picture back in 1972, they began praying for "that little girl." They had been haunted by the image of a small child running naked up the road, being chased by an inferno.
>
> By this point in time, I had laid perhaps thousands of questions at God's feet regarding the whys of my situation.
>
> I had simply been in the wrong place at the wrong time. But as to the greater meaning behind my pain, for so long I had been in the dark. And yet here were so many people telling me that my picture had prompted

them to pray. Had my suffering actually been the catalyst to bring me into God's family? Could such a thing be true?

In my heart, I knew the answer. *Those bombs led me to Christ.* Armed with that information, my passion soared for helping others make the connection between their pain and God's ultimate plan. (Phuc, 256–57)

## Chapter 20
# MOTHER EARTH'S MESSAGE

I once dreamed of some children who lived with their mother, who devoted a lot of time to making sure their home was a safe environment for them. However, the children were constantly quarreling with each other. Due to envy, misunderstanding, and selfishness, one child was mad at his brother and tore up his bed, damaged his desk, and broke the windows, which caused the brother to retaliate by torching his brother's room. They loved their mother but could not tolerate each other. They did not see the grief they caused their mother when they acted out of anger and hatred. The mother came home and saw one bedroom on fire and another bedroom torn apart. She cried and silently tried her best to repair the damage. Her children's lack of respect for each other pierced her heart.

Then I was taken to another scenario in which I saw Mother Earth as a body that was suffering and dying because of cancer caused by selfishness and power that was killing her vital organs—animals, humans, plants, soil, resources, water, and so on. The viruses had damaged her respiratory system, and she was suffocating because of air pollution. She had problems with her digestive system because of all the chemical and toxic wastes in her. I saw terrible signs of her cardiovascular system due to all the pressure in her veins that were blocked or ruptured because of economic, political, and social tensions. In Mother Earth, the people were infected by the selfishness virus (S-virus) and the power virus (P-virus) that made them arrogant, ignorant, irresponsible, and reckless. They were like zombies who went viral and infected others with selfishness and a lust for power. These viruses spread fast because they are media borne. With one click from anywhere, the toxic data reach the entire world and infect people's brains and emotional states.

Suddenly, I found myself in a community where people were suffering from a water shortage. Powerful and wealthy people had built a dam to control the water though they represented just 10 percent of the population. I saw how water would flow into a reservoir. I was instructed to throw a pebble into it to break the dam and release the water for all the people. I did not understand that, but I threw a pebble into the reservoir. The ripples it released moved a leaf, which knocked a branch down into the water, which bumped a boulder into the water, and so on. My pebble initiated a chain of events that ultimately burst the dam.

I feel that Mother Earth and Father Cosmos were telling me, "We are facing a serious problem in our house. There are four groups operating here—violators, onlookers, victims, and doers. The violators abuse others, cause destruction, and create problems. The onlookers do not know what to do; they are ignorant people who may or may not act as needed. The victims suffer from calamities, are trapped by adverse circumstances, and are wounded by hateful attacks. The doers have the ability to act, the knowledge to act accordingly, and the courage to act decisively. Facing the imminent danger caused by the violators, the doers act while the onlookers hesitate and the victims remain helpless. Just one of four groups can do anything, and it may not be enough to save the house."

Ninety percent of humankind is under the control of the 10 percent—the elites, policy makers, and rulers. Our fate lies in the hands of the capitalists, politicians, and scientists. They indoctrinate us with many ideas, philosophies, principles, and theories. They teach us the way we should interact, learn, think, and work. They set boundaries, guidelines, and rules for the rest of us.

I wish to unite all my brothers and sisters who are consciously aware of this fact as well as the imminent threat we face. We should combine our capacities, experiences, skills, and resources to heal

Mother Earth; we are all a part of her. Some of us can feel her anguish and hear her cry. We are the living cells in Mother Earth. Unfortunately, destructive and infectious cells cause problems to her body and threaten our survival. We should unite to boost Mother Earth's recovery rate and minimize the damage instead of directly or indirectly causing more injuries or spreading more problems by being onlookers, victims, or violators.

Many responsible doers are consciously and diligently trying to help Mother Earth, and they have made tremendous progress, but we are collectively facing a powerful giant. The times are turbulent and dangerous because our Mother Earth and the human race might be annihilated. I hope we are conscious enough to see beyond our differences and concentrate on helping Mother Earth and repairing our global home.

Regarding the way to handle the S-virus and P-virus, in a vision, I saw a table and referred to it as the selfishness and power-driven (SPD) table. We can build a strong defense against the S-virus and P-virus depending on how much we can control or manage our SPD table. Our levels of SPD can control us. We have the various levels of immunity to these viruses. For example, if our SPD level is 0 percent, the immunity number would be 100 percent. This is when we become spiritual beings because we no longer have bodies and there is 0 percent of selfish and power-driven elements in us. However, if we are 100 percent selfish and power-driven, we will become destructive humans because our actions and thinking processes will involve only aggression, ego, envy, impulse, and pride; our immunity is 0 percent because we do not know how to handle selfishness and power.

Gradually, we can reach 30 percent immunity, but we will still be heavily influenced and driven by selfishness and the desire for power making us ignorant and immature humans. When we reach 50 percent immunity, we will still struggle with selfishness and power issues.

Here is the scale that was shown to me in a vision.

| SPD Level | Immunity | Description |
|---|---|---|
| 0 percent | 100 percent | Spiritual Beings |
| 30 percent | 70 percent | Conscious and Responsible Humans |
| 50 percent | 50 percent | Ordinary Humans |
| 70 percent | 30 percent | Ignorant and Immature Humans |
| 0 percent | 100 percent | Destructive Humans |

Selfishness and Power Driven (SPD) Table

The ideal number would be 30 percent selfishness because we need to think of ourselves, our families, and our people as a foundation so we can extend our capacity to help others. We need to be power driven 30 percent because we will need power to survive, move forward, take a stand, and resist temptations. The 30 percent number would act as a system checkpoint because it reminds us of our vulnerability and weakness; we need to be diligent about keeping our immunity at 70 percent if we want to be conscious and responsible humans.

We want to avoid painful afflictions, shattered dreams, lost lives, broken promises, and other difficult issues, but we cannot always do that. If we are in a desert, we are bound to get sand on us. My tough experiences actually did me more good than harm. I came to realize that they were the potent and powerful ingredients I needed to enhance my strength of faith as I developed the art of resiliency. We benefit more from adversity than we do from prosperity. When we are prosperous and successful, we can easily be influenced by arrogance, complacency, greed, and selfishness, but when we face adverse situations, we develop the strengths of faith, resiliency, and compassion. Tough times give me the necessary vitamins that increase my compassion, strengthen my resiliency, and broaden my knowledge.

I pray that each reader's journey will be fruitful after receiving a certain word or idea just as a tiny piece of ash is enough to spark the fire of personal compassion, wisdom, and courage.

PART VI

## Chapter 21
# THE FIRST TEST

In Vietnam, a common saying is *Thất Bại là Mẹ Thành Công,* "Failure is the mother of success." Let us consider the example of Eve, the mother of humanity, and her failure in the Garden of Eden (Genesis 2:4–24, 3:1–13).

God created Adam and Eve and gave them the perfect Garden of Eden. God created everything with good intentions, and each of His creations had a purpose for its existence.

Because of His love, God gave the humans total freedom, but He wanted to monitor their maturity and wisdom. To do that, He created cunning Lucifer, Satan, whose mission was to attack, deceive, and tempt them. God gave Adam and Eve one command: "You may surely eat of every tree of the garden, but of the tree of the knowledge of good and evil you shall not eat, for in the day that you eat of it you shall surely die" (Genesis 2:16–17 ESV).

Unfortunately, as soon as God singled out the Tree of the Knowledge of Good and Evil, it became the center Adam's and Eve's attention. If our parents tell us we can play in any room except the attic, we will focus on getting into the attic and not care about the other rooms. If God had not told Adam and Eve about the Tree of the Knowledge of Good and Evil, perhaps they would not have paid any attention to it. However, there was the danger that they might have accidentally eaten the fruit of this tree, so being a responsible parent, God warned them about the danger.

Satan tested and put doubt, fear, temptation, and conflicting thoughts into the minds of Adam and Eve, and they failed. God allows us to choose, and even though we make mistakes, He helps us learn so we can evolve.

The primary objective of an AI designer is to create an operating system that can make smart decisions itself. The best way to achieve this is to give challenging tests or put the system in difficult situations to monitor how it handles them. This was a part of the design. God created good and evil. Imagine Him as a software programmer who designed and built a system. To test the system, He created bugs or viruses and allowed them to infiltrate and damage the data.

Our brains cannot handle the entire system file—God's knowledge or cosmic wisdom. The designer knows the system's limits and sets parameters necessary to prevent this problem. In the same way, God knew the danger and forbade them to eat fruit from the Tree of the Knowledge of Good and Evil. Perhaps it was a symbolic way of describing the concept of accessing and downloading information from the cosmic network. When the system security was breached, all access was denied. Since that time, humans have lost their connection to the cosmic network. We can use the example of a network key to gain access to a secured network system to understand this concept.

It was a clever design because the serpent—Satan, or perhaps our egos—gave Eve a persuasive argument: "You will not surely die. For God knows that when you eat of it your eyes will be opened, and you will be like God, knowing good and evil" (Genesis 3:4–5 ESV). The humans did not really respect God; they preferred to listen to the serpent and disobey God's one command meant to keep them safe. We may not be able to regain this level of trust because of the negative experiences and memories that haunt, damage, and hurt us. God is ready to trust His children again, however, no matter how many times they have broken this trust. God created us and knows how immature, vulnerable, and weak we are.

God trusted the first humans to keep the energetic harmony in the Garden of Eden. The commandment not to eat the fruit of that one tree was a contract between the first humans and God that Eve broke. She knew it as she told God, "The serpent deceived me, and I ate" (Genesis 3:13 ESV). We surmise that God would not have been surprised because by design, Adam and Eve were the first humans and Satan was created to be the most cunning deceiver. Eve was like an innocent village girl on her first visit to the big city who trusted crooks with her money. Her failure started a chain reaction that started evolution. If Adam and Eve had obeyed God, they could have lived in the garden happily ever after, but the learning cycle would never have started.

We have to see both sides of the coin, however. The only way the serpent could complete its task was to destroy the peace and harmony in the garden. Therefore, in one synchronized move, God allowed both creatures to learn and evolve. Humans progressed and survived while the serpent constantly challenged and destroyed.

We can learn not to repeat Eve's mistake; we have already lived through the mistakes of selfishness and power, so we should not repeat them. We can pray to God and ask for blessings or guidance, but when we hear God's words, we do not always follow them. We do not trust God. We act as children who have selective hearing; we tune in to the more favorable advice we want to hear and ignore advice we consider too strict. We have only a selective trust in God because we neglect to think of God when we are enjoying life even if we are warned to be more conscious of what we do. However, when we fall and lose everything, we tune in and place our trust in God. For this reason, we need to establish a balance so that during good and bad times alike, we will always have the same level of trust in God. We must mend the broken trust between God and us by living in a responsible manner.

By relating the parable of the Prodigal Son (Luke 15:11–32), to His disciples, Jesus was trying to share his perspective on the grand scheme of things. One son was obedient while the other was impulsive and immature. The father knew his sons and understood that the best way to learn was through failure. When the younger son admitted his mistakes, he demonstrated that he had learned a lesson. The older son defied his father by refusing to attend the party held to celebrate his brother's return; though he was the good son, he was affected by selfishness and power. He thought he should have been treated better than his younger brother after he returned home.

Perhaps the bad son's repentance is more noticeable than the good son's obedience. The bad son realized his mistake and learned his lesson, and he came back with the will to change. He did not expect to be treated as a son and was willing to be a servant in the house. On the other hand, the good son was always obedient and worked very hard to please his father. As humans, however, we know that we usually have an ulterior motive for being obedient and working hard to please someone. Here, he expected something in return, and he pleaded his case as he refused to enter the house to celebrate at his younger brother's party. If the older brother had really been a good son, he would have reacted just as his father had when his brother returned. Selfishness and power are the roots of all human conflict, hatred, suffering, and war.

Those of us with children can relate to this story because we have to deal with them every day. We have to be clear with them especially when the obedient ones are not happy or do not agree with the way we handle disobedient ones. We have to consider the big picture, one that includes everybody in the house. Using the analogy of a system design, we must look at the integrity of the program and try not to be caught by the data error incidents; we try to point out to the children how each one can connect and contribute to benefit the entire system. When they begin to see the big picture, they will put aside their differences and contribute for the benefit of the family. Parents can learn how to develop their management skills and experience success after failure.

When we focus on our spiritual paths, we often believe the purpose is to clear our karmic debts or to try to create merits and blessings for our children and grandchildren. These are some factors that Buddhist monks use to explain the spiritual path and to encourage us to try to follow it. However, when we really go deeper on the spiritual path, we see that our understanding is so different from what we thought we knew when we were young. After a big failure or life crisis, some of us were fortunate enough to learn more about spirituality.

Our souls, like tiny specks of light, combine with our bodies and represent parts of the Creator, a gigantic source of light. The soul uses the body as its instrument in the material world to learn and evolve. Because we are an element of this gigantic light source, our souls comes down to this material world without any sin or karma. It is like software than can be transferred from one piece of hardware to another. The software program is not good or bad in that it does not create good or bad data files; its users create good or bad data under positive or negative circumstances.

Our bodies are limited to a period of eighty to a hundred years or so; when we die, our souls migrate to other bodies to continue their journey. One life can be chaotic and sinful while the next might be peaceful. Maybe we will learn lessons that will allow us to live righteous lives and help our family members and others with the blessings we receive. These scenarios are not karma; they are just lessons that every soul must learn and pass through. However, in Buddhism, monks use the concept of karma as a way to teach us to avoid evil and always do good. Blessings and good karma are only the lessons and tests designed to measure our level of spiritual development. When we reach a sufficient level, we will be able to draw in and handle karma because we know these are the precious opportunities that our bodies and souls utilize while learning to apply the knowledge and experience we have obtained.

With such wisdom, we can easily transform karma into blessings. We can convert tragic incidents into wonderful opportunities to develop spiritually. Some of us have undergone transformation through personal experiences; perhaps God saved our lives and then guided us so we could share our experience with others and show them that we all have the ability to achieve everything just as divine beings such as Jesus and the Buddha did when they were on earth as humans.

One of our greatest errors is thinking that only holy or chosen people can be perfect, without sin, and righteous enough to gain enlightenment. It is wrong for us to think that because we are ordinary, lowly people, we will never attain enlightenment. Some condemn those who display godlike characters as being blasphemous and argue that humans cannot be equals of the divine beings. We do not try to be boastful or show disrespect by claiming to be the Buddha, Jesus Christ, or saints. We want to draw attention to the fact that divine beings are very righteous with unconditional love for us, the children of God. The divine beings wanted to demonstrate to humans their capacity to develop and evolve to reach the divine level and help others do the same. We must not be too selfish and greedy and strive to control this earth.

We cause problems and damage the cycles of evolution for other living creatures through our reckless and foolish actions. Due to pride and confusion in the darkness of uncertainty, we have caused severe damage to the earth. Chaotic and unstable social structures and a total loss of freedom in human lifestyles mean that our minds can never have peace because they are bombarded by preoccupations, concerns, thoughts, and fears. Due to humankind's uncontrollable greed, we are destroying the natural environment, which causes holes in the ozone layer, alters the climate, and affects our physical health. We dump all kinds of toxic waste into the oceans or bury it, and as a result, our sources of food are contaminated. We have created weapons of mass destruction and now have to confront this deadly threat. We wonder how the divine beings, the parents of all living creatures, can close their eyes and let us be harmed.

Reading scripture makes us aware that the divine beings have promised to return to help save all living creatures. Now is the moment they return to earth in human forms to help the world during this critical period. They have wise bodies and enlightened souls who can do things beyond our imagination. They come as role models who give us hope in our desperate situations.

Because of pride, we think we are intelligent enough to control our situations. Only when we face circumstances that threaten our survival and feel helpless and desperate will the real saviors appear, and we will know their abilities are not from the material world. Who thinks they would survive a major biological, chemical, or nuclear war? Where could we run with our loved ones?

During such a critical moment, we will discover the potential of our GPA. We can understand some people's disbelief of that because in the past, we were very skeptical as well. However, when we witnessed and became aware of God's amazing capability, we realized how ignorant we were. The reality is totally beyond human perception and imagination because we were capable only of evaluations that used the nearsighted observations of our brains. As we grew more in faith, we became enlightened and more capable of understanding further and deeper the wonderful and lively hands of God working through our lives. We came to know and believe that no matter how humans try to destroy each other by deploying their advanced technologies, the divine beings still had a solution to save and transform us.

Humankind causes so much of the chaos, problems, and suffering on earth because of our greed and selfishness. We caused terrible damage to the environment, and the consequences of our actions were sudden changes that cost human lives. Then we blamed it on Mother Nature and criticized the divine beings for allowing these events to happen. Humans hurt and kill each other, but the divine beings never want to harm their children. We are living in the twenty-first century, the age of advanced science. We will learn which side—the destroyers or the savers of life—will tip the balance in this final trial. Scientists, politicians, capitalists, and religious leaders have plans to control or destroy humanity. We will see if they have the power to save themselves when they must face the consequences of their actions. Contamination due to viruses, chemical agents, and nuclear radiation have caused the unjust deaths of countless souls who died in vain and full of hatred and despair; they are still wandering the earth waiting to be liberated. These things are examples of the problems for which humankind awaits solutions. Many people have made predictions and have seen solutions, which is why they are less concerned and fearful and more confident and happy.

## Chapter 22
# THE FINAL EXAM

One time, I dreamed about the final judgment. The Lord used a theater to help me understand this concept. In this scenario, I saw a director, actors, stagehands, makeup artists, and others getting ready to stage a play. The director gave scripts to the actors, who learned their roles. The play's plot had many twists and turns. At the end of the play, the actors met with the director to go over their performances. This is one way of understanding the final judgment.

I learned about the end times and the final judgment from the Bible; we will all take this final exam at the end of the course, at the end of our lives, to determine whether we pass or fail. This exam will be the most difficult test just as Jesus Christ warned us.

> For then there will be great tribulation, such as has not been from the beginning of the world until now, no, and never will be. (Matthew 24:21 ESV)

> Pray that it may not happen in winter. For in those days there will be such tribulation as has not been from the beginning of the creation that God created until now, and never will be. (Mark 13: 18–19 ESV)

I think of it as the final exam before human beings can attain a new level. After passing this exam, we will complete this period of learning through suffering, and there will no longer be disease, famine, tribulation, or war. This is the vision of John.

> Then I saw a new heaven and a new earth, for the first heaven and the first earth had passed away, and the sea was no more. And I saw the holy city, new Jerusalem, coming down out of heaven from God, prepared as a bride adorned for her husband. And I heard a loud voice from the throne saying, "Behold, the dwelling place of God is with man. He will dwell with them, and they will be his people, and God himself will be with them as their God. He will wipe away every tear from their eyes, and death shall be no more, neither shall there be mourning, nor crying, nor pain anymore, for the former things have passed away." (Revelation 21: 1–4 ESV)

Based on Matthew 25:31–41 and Revelation 20:10–15, at the final judgment, some will be sent to the lake of fire for eternal punishment. I do not believe God will condemn the souls of His immature children and especially those who did not know Him and were blasphemous, defiant, ignorant, sinful, and unfaithful. Would God punish and condemn them forever? I do not think so because of the way Jesus Christ said on the cross: "Father, forgive them, for they know not what they do" (Luke 23:34 ESV).

When we were toddlers and teenagers, we did not really know our fathers and mothers. We knew they were there 24/7 to prepare our meals, take care of us, give us orders, and scold us. Many times, we felt distant from them, defiant, and angry because we did not understand why they were being so strict with us. I was hurt and devastated when I lost everything after the fatal car crash on 04/13/1990. I did not understand God's intentions, so I was very angry and defiant. My soul should have been scolded or punished severely when I met God, but He decided to give me another chance by assigning me a job.

It is not the nature of a merciful, responsible, and wise Father to send these children to eternal torment. He knew that they were immature and inexperienced and that He had given them free will; He knew that they would make mistakes. Being a merciful and responsible Father, He will do anything to help His lost children and will not condemn them to eternal torment. I will never abandon my children even if they defy or hurt me because I know they are a part of me. If I abandon or condemn them, I am abandoning and condemning myself. If I think like that, I know God can see much more.

Jesus gave us the encouraging story of the lost sheep.

> What do you think? If a man has a hundred sheep, and one of them has gone astray, does he not leave the ninety-nine on the mountains and go in search of the one that went astray? And if he finds it, truly, I say to you, he rejoices over it more than over the ninety-nine that never went astray. So it is not the will of my Father who is in heaven that one of these little ones should perish. (Matthew 18:12–14 ESV)

> What man of you, having a hundred sheep, if he has lost one of them, does not leave the ninety-nine in the open country, and go after the one that is lost, until he finds it? And when he has found it, he lays it on his shoulders, rejoicing. And when he comes home, he calls together his friends and his neighbors, saying to them, "Rejoice with me, for I have found my sheep that was lost." Just so, I tell you, there will be more joy in heaven over one sinner who repents than over ninety-nine righteous persons who need no repentance. (Luke 15:4–7 ESV)

The final judgment will be an overall evaluation so each soul can obtain a clear perspective on its learning curve and more important on God's love and wisdom. This will be the final assessment of the system's performance and its data, network speed, and integrity. I see God's final judgment as His self-evaluation. Since God created us in His image, He knows our levels of wisdom and behavioral patterns. As a loving and responsible parent, He gave us free will and trusted His design that no matter what we chose, in the end, everyone would benefit. He will review all souls to complete their learning.

God created us to learn and evolve. We start out as inexperienced and vulnerable novices, but we can advance to the intermediate level in which we have some experience but are still immature and weak. At the advanced level, we have gained enough experience to be more mature and responsible.

The idea of the final judgment is a scare tactic to remind people to do good and avoid evil. Jesus told us that there were many rooms in His Father's house (John 14:2). Certainly, there is a dark region in God's kingdom, a dark closet or a time-out place in the house where parents send their disobedient and naughty children to discipline them, but as a loving parent, God does not rest until all His children are home.

Because of selfishness and power struggles, we experience aggression, evil, hatred, injustice, terrorism, and violence, and the victims of these evils do not seem to have a voice. These souls have been crying out to God, "O Sovereign Lord, holy and true, how long before you will judge and avenge our blood on those who dwell on the earth?" (Revelation 6:10 ESV). Many people are struggling and suffering and are trapped in abusive homes, toxic workplaces, and violent neighborhoods. The people who commit these acts will face the consequences as their souls are in the dark region to reflect on what they have done.

Some souls have been in the dark abyss from the dawn of time. Though they have been in this dark region for millions of years, their cases are not as severe as the cases of those who have gone there recently. Our earliest ancestors did not have in-depth knowledge of God's laws or presence, so God would not severely punish them for aggression, blasphemy, killing, and stealing. However, as humankind became more mature especially during the past four or five centuries with the development of advanced educational, scientific, and social systems, we should have better understanding of our actions and suffer greater punishment for our bad actions. It is not God who judges them; in fact, their consciousness acts as a mirror reflection of what they have done. Since they already knew that but still committed those acts because of distractions, ignorance, and temptation, they judge themselves harshly.

Being a loving and responsible parent, God sends advanced souls to this dark region to help and save those who are trapped there without hope. Imagine that your parents count on you to help your younger brothers and sisters, but one rebellious brother leaves home and becomes lost and homeless. Your father asks you to go look for him. Your immature brother may still hold the grudge against his father, but he accepts you. Similarly, immature and inexperienced souls may not know or accept God, but He still loves them. God will assign advanced souls to help these lost or immature ones in the dark region because they can relate to each other. Therefore, when a soul is assigned or volunteers to go to the dark region, it does not suffer torment but will feel the fear, sorrow, and torture of the others in the dark region. This soul comes as the indirect hand of God to bring His grace and love to souls who are in the darkness. God saved my life and assigned me to witness His grace and love. I volunteered to be sent to the hell to help suffering souls there.

Missionaries volunteered to go to unknown regions in Africa, America, and Asia in the sixteenth and seventeenth centuries. These missionaries had to live among the local people to relate to them and teach them about Christianity.

On the spiritual path, after souls reach the advanced level and have gained experience and wisdom, they will realize that others are still struggling and trapped in the physical world or in hell. With compassion, wisdom, and courage, these souls would ask God to go down to help them, and God would gladly give these souls the help they needed to do the job effectively. Gradually, these volunteer souls will turn the most terrible or unhappy area in God's kingdom into a loving, peaceful place. As John wrote, "Behold, the dwelling place of God is with man. He will dwell with them, and they will be his people, and God himself will be with them as their God" (Revelation 21:3 ESV).

After this final exam, we will reach a new level and condition. There will not be any chaos, disease, sin, suffering, or war because all will have God's presence in them, will live in harmony with God, and will focus on their assignments and missions. Using my example of the school, after passing the finals to graduate from college, we will not need to study calculus, chemistry, history, or English composition anymore.

## Chapter 23
# MY MISSING KEYS STORY

One night, I searched for my keys as I was about to leave for work but could not find them though I knew they were in the house somewhere. I had to borrow my wife's spare keys to go to work. While I was driving to work, I retraced my steps to remember where I had left my keys. That mental exercise continued throughout my shift and then on my way home. In the middle of this ordeal, I received a meaningful message: "You spent energy looking for your keys, tools you need to commute to work and enter your house. You do not think about them when you have them, but you cannot get them out of your mind when they're missing. Just imagine if this was about someone you loved who went missing; you would frantically search for him or her. Now imagine how much more God, with His infinite abilities and wisdom, would search for and help His children who were lost or trapped."

As soon as I received this message, I knew why my keys had gone missing. When I got home, I immediately went to the places I thought I could have left them and found them at the bottom of my backpack though I had searched it several times the previous night. That incident gave me a profound insight; I realized that some times when I think someone is lost, that person is actually right next to me though I hadn't realized that. That is human nature.

The moral of this story is that God never abandons His children and that He goes to great lengths to save all the lost ones. It gave me a boost of hope and a stronger faith; if I could exert a great deal of energy to look for my missing keys, God can certainly expend His power on helping His lost children find their way. The missing keys story is the key to my resilient power.

# PART VII

## Chapter 24
# THE SUN WILL SHINE AFTER THE RAIN

The conditions of earth and humanity have reached critical limits. We cannot continue down this destructive path living with a false sense of peace and security and ignorant of or ignoring all the damage we have indirectly or directly caused. Maybe it is too harsh to judge all humans for this mistake since only a small percentage of the world's population, maybe 10 percent, is responsible for our current situation. These elites have money, power, and intelligence; they are the capitalists, politicians, and scientists; they, our policy makers, dictate how we live. Under the guise of freedom, justice, and equality, they design systems that rule the rest of humanity as if they were children.

It is important for everybody to know the level of influence our collective consciousness has. By looking at one of the normal functions from our daily behaviors, we can gauge the level of our collective consciousness. We simply need to observe people's driving habits and we will see some go through red lights causing us to slam on our brakes. Multiply such irresponsible incidents by the millions of drivers on the road and we can see how such behavior can have a big effect on our society. In contrast, by raising the level of the collective consciousness, we will become more responsible and less stressed out. To illustrate the concept of the collective consciousness, consider how many more people have to die or suffer before we raise public awareness of the dangers of DUI.

Humanity would truly have freedom, justice, and equality if

everybody acted in a conscious and responsible manner for the sake of our world and the future. Many people think that acquiring money, fame, and power is the primary objective of life. They can be very ambitious, devious, greedy, ignorant, and reckless and do almost anything to achieve their goals. Capitalists are interested only in getting rich; they ignore the environmental pollution and public health hazards caused by their products, and they formulate cover-up tactics so they can continue to conduct their profitable businesses. In the same manner, politicians use the media as a propaganda tool to rally the people with many promises. Then, when they are in power, they have a totally different agenda that may not be beneficial to the people. However, using their authority and political schemes, they keep the people in the dark.

Most of us tend to believe whatever scientists claim. Currently, scientists will say that it is safe to use a product, so we naturally follow their advice. However, months or years later, they will issue another report stating that it is now unsafe to use the product. Again, we have to listen to them and stop using the product. Through these examples of the status quo, we realize that the fate of our world rests in the hands of capitalists, politicians, and scientists who are acting in their own best interests. If they combined their resources and capabilities for the sake of humanity, the social system could work and we could enjoy freedom, justice, and equality, but that is a big "if" because at the moment, seeing all the pollution, contamination, famine, global warming, natural disasters, and pandemics and despite the divine messages asking us to change our way of living, the rich and powerful do not seem to care or even pay attention. They continue to conduct business as usual and let the rest of us suffer.

Those who are ignorant, immature, irresponsible, shortsighted, and stubborn will have to learn a lesson. We all live together in the same house—earth. We hope for a brighter and better world and a future in which we will see no more suffering.

Humankind has experienced the horrors of the Black Death and other epidemics. We have lived through turbulent periods such as the holy wars and world wars. We have seen the destructive power of nuclear bombs and biological and chemical weapons. In the past, humanity had to deal with only one of these dangers at a time to observe and learn the extent of its ability to cause damage. Now, these dangers are converging and can happen simultaneously. Terrorists have developed biological, chemical, and nuclear weapons of mass destruction and are waiting for the right moment to strike. The World Health Organization is worried about the possibility of a pandemic. Since the 2004 tsunami in Southeast Asia, there have been more natural disasters such as earthquakes, hurricanes, tornadoes, and volcanic activity that have caused global fear and alarm. We can only hope and pray that through the many storms, humanity will become more conscious, mature, and enlightened and make our world a better place for all creatures to live and evolve according to the divine plan.

## Chapter 25
# THE SURVIVING PRISONER STORY

One of my father's friends, whom I will simply call Uncle T, was in the Republic of Vietnam Air Force. He could not leave South Vietnam when the Communists took over on April 30, 1975. Being a high-ranking air force officer, he was sent to a reeducation camp somewhere in the north. Basically, he was serving a slow death sentence as he was tortured and sent to do hard labor in the deep jungle. Somehow, he survived ten years there and miraculously made his way to the United States. He visited us in 1990 when I was working as a senior applications engineer in Santa Clara, California. He told us about the difficult challenges he had faced after the Communists took over and how he thought his fate had been sealed. As we exchanged ideas on the concept of fate, I shared my view from the perspective of a software programmer. I said, "I believe I am in control of my own fate and destiny because when I constantly select the best options or good information to make a decision, it is similar to software that analyzes and picks the data input to give the most effective or beneficial output. So when I carefully select the data input with my best decision-making abilities, I believe that the output will be under my control and that I am in charge of my fate."

Uncle T told me something I did not fully agree with at the time, but it turned out to be prophetic: "I used to think like you especially when I had everything back then. I had power and skills as a high-ranking officer in the air force. But all the money, power, and skills I had could not do anything for me when I was desperate and helpless in the reeducation camp. In prison, I discovered God, who saved me and gave me freedom."

I heard what he said, but I still held onto my belief that I was in control of my fate. God was fair because He had brought this man who had to endure ten years in a Communist prison to give me a reminder, but I did not listen. I still remember what I had heard in the ER after my car accident: *You plan things, but I make things happen!* At that point, I knew my fate was sealed and my faith was fixed. I have always remembered this brief conversation prior to the point that I had to face the reality that I had no control over my fate, destiny, career, or life. Whenever I was in a turbulent storm due to blindness, distractions, mistakes, or weakness, I always hit my reset button, put myself right back in the ER, and heard this reminder again. I would ask myself in any stressful or hopeless situation, *How can it get any worse than a body in the dark emergency room? You have faced the angel of death and almost lost!* There is a very encouraging sign that God really makes things happen, and I am a living proof of His amazing grace. There are many wonderful testimonies out there just like this surviving prisoner story to let us know that God loves His children unconditionally.

After several sessions on the God-presence energy (GPE) training course, one day, a powerful thought came to me. This is the way I felt and wrote down to express to the Lord.

## The Important Values of Humility and Patience

31 August 2020
Dear Lord,

I have been meditating on many thoughts I have received from You. I decided to express my gratitude in this letter to remind everyone of the way You teach us the values of humility and patience. You have opened my heart and mind and planted the seed of Your presence in me, which has grown to the point that it dominates my thinking and fills my mind with thoughts and visions.

For more than a week, I have received many explanations or ideas, and they were about the God-presence seed (the GP seed). You gave me a deeper understanding of the importance of being humble and patient. Many pieces of information come to my mind, and I try my best to present them here in a chronological order to thank You for the knowledge and support You have given me and to write down what I have perceived so You can evaluate and guide me by providing indirect feedback from the people who read this.

## Becoming the GP Seed

I once dreamed I was a tiny seed buried in earth. Though I was a tiny seed, I still had consciousness and sensory systems. I felt the pressure and the weight of the earth because I was buried very deeply. I recognized the presence of insects and worms, but I could not move. Suddenly, I realized that as a seed, I had the potential to grow even though I could not move. Then I was transported back to the current state of being and observed a seed that You planted deeply in my subconscious. The insects, worms, and weeds were forms of doubt, fear, ignorance, power, selfishness, and temptation. You have shown me a very profound point in which You reminded me of the GP seed. This GP seed contains the full capacity of Your creative power and infinite wisdom. The GP seed can be a brilliant idea or profound thought that is sown in the mind. The seed may grow if I take it seriously and work diligently to transform a neuron firing into a verbal statement. This is the first stage in which I am convinced that it will come true, and I am determined to make it happen. You have taught me that each person does not have to see the encouraging signs or positive results to know the capacities of this seed because as he or she reaches the GPE level of 90 percent or higher, he or she becomes the GP seed.

You opened hearts and minds and planted GP seeds in everyone so all could learn to be still and let them grow. We have worries, fears, and thoughts that overwork our brains and deplete our energy. We need to park our minds and be still. You have shown me a vision of a loving parent who wants to teach toddlers and teenagers. As toddlers, we were distracted, restless, and silly. As teenagers, we were defiant, ignorant, impatient, and stubborn. Therefore, we could not be still enough to listen or observe what our parent wished to pass on to us. When we matured, we came to appreciate the values of being still and listening to what our parents had tried to teach us.

I am blessed and honored that You let me see things from Your point of view. I see chaos, injustice, and transgression, but You see all the tiny pieces of the big puzzle. Only You can decide to let something take place that can be a good lesson for immature souls and become an invaluable opportunity for experienced souls. People cannot see this depth and for sure do not have Your knowledge to make these impactful decisions.

You showed me a vision of a toddler and teenager. The toddler really wanted his brother's favorite toy car. While his brother was not home, he asked his father to get the toy car in his brother's room. With the father's permission, he took the toy to play with, but he was not careful, and he broke it. His brother was very angry at him but was more upset that his father had allowed the younger brother to take his toy. The father knew that the toddler needed to learn a lesson as he actually felt bad because he had broken the toy that he and his brother really liked. It was also an opportunity for the teenager to realize that brotherly relationships are worth more than a toy.

Through this example, You revealed to me the different levels of understanding. The toddler's only interest was the toy, and he would not understand anything else the father tried to tell him. The teenager believed he knew everything and might not listen to his father's advice and guidance. The father knew his children's levels of understanding and felt responsible for their growth and well-being. Certainly, the father had the ability to guide and help his children; in this example, the father could have easily resolved the problem by buying the favorite toys for both children.

You are our divine parent who has abundant grace and love. One tiny speck of Your grace or love would be more than enough to calm turbulent storms or violent aggression. I can compare the hidden potential of Your grace and love to the nuclear energy in an atom. I use the concept of the GPE's radiation effect to describe the deep impact of Your grace and love.

## Humility and Patience

Humility gives us total access to the knowledge base because we really appreciate and value people's opinions and viewpoints. Since we humbly and respectfully listen to others, we actually download everything. It is the ego or power struggles that cause us to be critical or discriminating and to limit ourselves. Patience lets us utilize the full range of time and observe its powerful effects. When we patiently wait for things to unfold, we weather storms and changing seasons and find the meaning of events. Through this process, we develop compassion, wisdom, and courage. Therefore, environments, adverse and favorable conditions, and external and internal circumstances are the necessary fertilizers for this GP seed.

Humankind needs to understand the essence of time because You have made it for a purpose. Days, nights, and seasons have special functions in Your grand design. Human beings are very arrogant, distracted, ignorant, and impatient. They want everything now, and in their minds, days are too short and nights are too long or vice versa. People rush through life and do not appreciate the precious moments You have given them through the good and bad times, the high and low points.

On my journey, even though there were many dark storms and turbulent times, You have taught me to be still so I could observe the movement of life, the synchronicity of nature, and Your precision. You have taught me the value of humility and patience by being with me and observing with me how the dark night transforms into dawn. Being a loving parent, You sat through the night with me and experienced my disappointments, fears, mistakes, temptations, and unrest. Through the lesson of being still, You have shown me the subtle voice of silence and its effective resonance.

I know I am sitting on top of an infinite treasure, but I need to work diligently to benefit from the hard-earned values of humility and patience. I believe You also reach out to many others and help them just as You have helped me. I want people to discover the benefit and potential of the GP seeds You have planted in us. Many people do not believe in or even know You because they simply do not have enough information, but they desperately need to know You. They need to be still to see You everywhere around them. We act like children who are restless and impatient and unable to be silent and listen to You.

You can open many doors of opportunity, but You allow me to experience the internal opening of the intuitive potential rather than the opening from the outside. The internal opening requires an open heart and mind, truthfulness, and humility by which we discover Your presence in and outside us. The opening from the outside is the case of somebody who helps open a person's mind's eye. In this process, a person can become dependent on the one who opens his or her mind's eye and is easily influenced by his or her mentor or master.

The first wave of GPE practitioners are blessed to experience how the seeds are planted and how they gradually go through the growth process. These GP seeds are different from other seeds. The growth of the other seeds will depend on the environments and soil in which they were planted. If the environment is not suitable or the soil is bad, these seeds might not grow to their full potential. However, the GP seed can change the environment or transmute the soul where it is planted in order to grow according to its potential. For example, a GP seed can be in a broken home, a bad community, or a strict culture, but it can convert these factors into fertilizer to promote growth. The seeds of the future generations of GPE practitioners will have much better growth because the soil has been fertilized by many experiences or results from the first or recent waves.

I praise You for the profound lessons of humility and patience because many people are struggling during this challenging and turbulent time in which everybody is covered by the dark cloud of danger, fear, isolation, and suffering.

My Lord, I make a solemn pledge to You that my soul will not rest or return home until I finish the assignments You have given me. I will stay in the dark abyss to help souls trapped there. Through grace and guidance, You have given unconditional love to my defiant, sinful, and weak soul. I am a seed that will be planted in the lowest depths of the dark abyss to be a witness to Your grace and love for all tormented souls. I commit to being Your instrument. You see through the depths of my heart and soul. You are my Maker, my Judge, and my Savior. There is nothing in the physical world or the spiritual realm that can stop my commitment and my trust in You, amen.

## The Voice of Silence

I have gone through the training to know the ability and essence of the voice of silence, one way God communicates and interacts with us. I need to be disciplined to hold my tongue and let God speak; I need to be still and let God intervene. We need to know how to gain access to God's subtle communications system because we do not have the ability to communicate directly with Him. We cannot hear or see God with our ears and eyes though throughout history, but some people could hear or see the divine beings; I believe God gave them those abilities.

St. Catherine of Siena listened and talked to God, but nobody else could hear Him. St. Bernadette Soubirous saw and talked to the Virgin Mary in Lourdes though the crowd could not see or hear anything. Francisco, Jacinta, and Lucia saw and talked to the holy Mother in Fatima while all the people around them saw and heard nothing.

I do not think God is hiding from His children. On the contrary, He is always present in and around us, but we are not looking for Him or listening to His silent voice. Just like children, we have selective hearing and tunnel vision, and we can be disobedient, ignorant, and reckless, but He is our loving and wise parent who constantly monitors His children and their environments.

Because we rely totally on our physical senses to interact with the world, we are easily distracted by material factors such as fame, fortune, and lust. Additionally, our brains are influenced and programmed by academic, cultural, political, religious, and social systems. The human race is under the control of the capitalists, politicians, and scientists who make the policies and rules. Therefore, our view is shortsighted and our minds are limited. We face imminent threats including climate change, mass extinction, pandemics, terrorism, and war because of selfishness and power struggles. During this critical time, God reaches out to help us open our minds' eyes to reality. God silently reaches out and reveals Himself to those who open their hearts and minds to His presence.

GPE is the voice of silence. You can raise its volume by increasing your GPE level to 70 percent or higher. At that range, God's presence will dominate your mind so your hearing and seeing abilities will be sharper. You will come up with ideas on what to do, and as you are about to act, the issues will be resolved and God will say to you silently, "I am way ahead of you!"

Let's say you are working on a project with your manager and you know exactly what to do in a certain situation and are prepared to act when it comes up. But as you step in to do the work, you find that your manager was already a step ahead and had everything resolved. This is my way of understanding the connection as we work together and know the status of the job. When a situation arises, we can act in sync with the manager. Therefore, as we constantly focus on developing our GPE, we will have a broader perspective that includes the alignment of heavenly timing, earthly advantage, and human harmony.

We can hear the difference between someone's loud voice and God's silent voice. Someone's loud voice might not reach across a large room, or it could be ignored. Because this person is boasting or sending a message to serve his selfish interests, it does not resonate well. On the other hand, God's silent voice will reach everybody on earth, and it penetrates hearts and minds.

Corresponding actions and phenomena follow God's voice to back up His words. God instructed Noah to build the ark, and He followed through with the great flood. God told Moses to ask the Pharaoh to let the Jews go or face the consequences, and He backed that up with ten plagues. We should focus our effort to find God's silent voice and learn to listen to it. Keep in mind that this is the voice of the Most High who created the universe. God's silent voice carries more weight than do those of all the powerful rulers on earth because He puts together heavenly timing, earthly advantage, and human harmony to make things happen.

When we follow God's instructions, we begin to discover the essence of the voice of silence. Jesus Christ constantly listened to God's silent voice and always said or did something at the right time, in the right place, and with the right people. For example, on the Sabbath, Jesus was in the synagogue and healed a sick person. He raised Lazarus from the dead in front of all the people who were there. Jesus has set the bar for us to know what He had accomplished because He actually encouraged us to do better: "Truly, truly, I say to you, whoever believes in me will also do the works that I do; and greater works than these will he do, because I am going to the Father. Whatever you ask in my name, this I will do, that the Father may be glorified in the Son" (John 14:12–13 ESV), and we will make His wish come true. We can express our gratitude by following the Lord's instruction with open hearts and minds, truthfulness, and humility.

At the GPE level of 70 percent or higher, we are very much in harmony with God's words and actions, and we sincerely and faithfully follow His will just as children who dearly love and trust their parents do. We really try to thrive and please our heavenly Father and make Him proud. This is the frame of mind we should have.

I leave this verse as a reminder for myself and others: "Wait for the Lord; be strong, and let your heart take courage; wait for the Lord!" (Psalm 27:14 ESV).

# PART VIII

## Chapter 26
# AN APPARENT TRAGEDY IS A HIDDEN BLESSING

When Vietnamese people face difficult trials, they encourage themselves and others by saying, *Trong họa có phúc*, "Every cloud has a silver lining." They try their best to get through their ordeals and learn from them for their and others' sakes and to help others avoid making the mistakes they have.

There is another way of looking at our failures and problems. We can think that perhaps it could be the residue of a past debt, unfinished business, or an unresolved issue. When we initiate an energy vibration, it continues to resonate. For instance, perhaps we had done something that created a strong energy vibration, and many years later, we had to face the consequences of our actions. Maybe it was an act of violence triggered by anger, which caused deep emotional and psychological wounds when we were young, and we have to confront it later after we have reached adulthood.

We can try to use Newton's third law of motion to understand the magnitude of this energetic resonance: "For every action there is an equal and opposite reaction."[4] Our crises might be a reaction to an action we took a long time ago. This mindset can help us endure the crisis instead of denying it and creating more negative vibrations.

By using this approach, we can try to adapt ourselves to the law of reciprocity in social psychology. Jesus said, "And as you wish that others would do to you, do so to them" (Luke 6:31 ESV). We know we

---

[4] https://www.physicsclassroom.com/class/newtlaws/Lesson-4/Newton-s-Third-Law.

have to pay our debts. I refer to the balancing of energy process, and I use the principle of "paying debt with respect," *trả nghiệp trong danh dự*. This is a very profound principle through which we learn not to blame others for our problems or trials especially when we are the victims. We focus our efforts on making the best of bad situations. We try to generate energy vibrations to balance out all the energy wavelengths that can occur in different forms such as interferences, blocks, and destructive forces. This principle goes deeper than the energetic vibration; in fact, it reaches all the way to the spiritual connections between all the people involved in this ordeal.

Let us use the example of the failed communication or incomplete data transmission to analyze the process by which we can efficiently handle it. Naturally, when we see a problem, we should realize that adjustments are needed. We examine the whole system and check the level of noise and interference because that may cause problems for our signal. We also look at the hardware such as the transmitter, receiver, and wires. One faulty device can cause the system to fail or malfunction. We even try to go deeper to see if there are problems with the actual message. In this case, we are checking syntax and semantics.

We also have to consider the synchronization between the two network systems. These considerations can help us to figure out what is wrong so we can modify the systems and fix the problem. This is a very mechanical way to show that it takes much effort on our end to improve a situation. In reality, when we have to synchronize the two network systems in the last step, we are talking about the problems that involve animosity between two sides. That being the case, we would find ourselves involved in a peace negotiation wherein our focus would be on balancing the energy vibrations coming from all the people around us especially when we are dealing with problems such as arguments, conflicts, and fights.

This suggestion helps us with the synchronization process. We should train our minds to consider the chance that there is at least one good thing we can gain out of ten bad things that happen to us. We should focus on looking for a person's positive side even though he or she might have made ten terrible mistakes. We should not focus on people's bad habits or mistakes in order to criticize or condemn them lest we keep such bad data in our minds and eventually become bad people.

By practicing the GPE meditation, we can learn to manage our energy frequencies as we interact with our environments. We can view space and time as components of energy, and by applying this idea, we can figure out a method to turn a moment of failure into an opportunity for success. A moment of failure, defeat, or loss can be a form of negative energy that can make us feel bad, unhappy, and upset. Depending on our level of perception, we can see it as either negative or positive. We can use the example of the expression "Get in the holiday spirit" to demonstrate this point.

During Christmas time, we Christians remember the blessings God has given us, and we have the opportunity to remind ourselves of this grace as we express our gratitude. This is typically done through songs of praise, sincere prayers, and acts of kindness. This atmosphere can get us into the holiday spirit. We develop a cheerful mindset that helps us be more affectionate, forgiving, generous, and understanding. We put our differences aside to bring joy and peace to one another during this time of the year.

However, when the holiday season is over, we tend to return to our negative ways. If we could maintain this atmosphere and mindset every day, just imagine how much we could change and what effect we would have throughout the year. Conversely, we should know that this atmosphere can also aggravate people's emotional wounds and pains. We feel very lonely and sad during the holiday season when we lose someone we dearly love. Therefore, it can be the amplifier that boosts people's joy or sorrow.

After my automobile accident in 1990, my mother gave me several CDs containing inspirational hymns I listened to during my recovery and mourning periods. As I was listening to these hymns next to my fiancée's grave during the first Christmas holiday, each word sank deeply into my heart and soul. At that moment, those words became my prayers because I could truly feel the author's sorrow and

God's loving grace alike. Now when I sing these hymns, I sense the vibration of a weak and vulnerable soul who is really reaching out to God as I had during that cold winter night at the cemetery. Now as before, in return comes the warm embrace of a loving God who touches a wounded heart.

When my heart is healed and my soul is very strong, I shed tears to express my gratitude in these silent prayers. We can relate to this idea through the feelings we have about our parents. They might have been tough disciplinarians when we were children, but when we mature, we develop an appreciation for their love including their discipline. Sometimes, we silently find ourselves shedding tears when we think of everything our parents did for us. St. Thérèse of Lisieux said, "When all the joys of Heaven come flooding into a human heart, how difficult it is for that heart, still in exile, to stand the strain of the impact without finding the relief in tears."[5] I have come to realize the wonderful meaning of prayer. I sang these hymns more than twenty years ago with tears of sorrow, but now I sing them with tears of joy because I feel God's love and grace.

Before a game, athletes can feel confident, enthusiastic, and full of energy, but if they lose, they can feel devastated, inferior, upset, vulnerable, and weak especially if it was a very close game. According to the energetic concept, all events can be defined as positive energy (+E) or negative energy (-E) events. Wins boost athletes' positive energy while losses boost athletes' negative energy.

Money can create a positive-energy event that generates more business opportunities and jobs, or it can create a negative-energy event that causes enmity and stress.

How can we turn rocks that were thrown onto our paths and cause us to stumble into diamonds that become the means to help us resurface the entire road?

In the following diagram, I provide the general concept (as shown in the diagram below) to explain how we can transform a moment of

---

[5] J. H. Adels, *The Wisdom of the Saints: An Anthology* (Oxford University Press, 1989), 189.

failure into an opportunity for success, a negative-energy event into a positive-energy event.

Transforming Negative Energy (-E) to Positive Energy (+E)

## NEGATIVE ENERGY (-E)

## POSITIVE ENERGY (+E)

Transforming a Misfortune into a Golden Opportunity

We can use the model of an I/O (input/output) device to understand this point. Let us consider the human body as the I/O device because we constantly receive and transmit various forms of energy. With this model, we can explore the dynamics of a simple interaction that takes place during a normal routine. When we are for instance cooking a meal, we can be very focused on all the details of the recipe and genuinely try to generate a positive energy input. But if we are distracted when we are cooking perhaps because we had had a bad day at work and we feel angry, careless, distracted, and just plain bad, our energy input is quite negative and our output will be negative. Taking the same approach, we can analyze our daily interactions in our businesses, communities, families, and other relationships.

We have to transform negative energy inputs, moments of failure, into positive energy outputs, opportunities for success. This transformation will require many steps during which we will need to develop patience, adaptability, wisdom, and trust. Our overall energy is negative when we are facing low points, moments of failure. We may have negative feelings such as depression, fear, and hopelessness, or we may be hurt, upset, and worried. These types of negative vibrations can affect our minds and bodies and eventually our lifestyles.

The GPE meditation practice can help us develop patience. As we learn and make progress, our capacity to endure our ups and downs goes up as a result of our regular practice of meditation to calm our minds. Additionally, we develop tolerance so we will be better able to accept situations in life. We also develop a higher level of adaptability as well as a knowledge base that will help us be more peaceful and see more clearly.

Gradually, as we gain wisdom based on this large knowledge base, we will gain the confidence we need to handle situations because we have a deep level of trust. Even if we are in a bad or desperate situation, we will know we can endure because we can accept the condition, we know what is going on, and we confidently believe that it is a transition to something better.

We can use this concept to build up our confidence and trust. Cosmic energy, or the life force, is the creative energy that connects all living creatures. Consider cosmic energy as an operating system that connects and controls devices; it ensures that the computer works efficiently. Functions such as file deletion, disk formatting, and defragmentation can be cumbersome, but they are necessary. Operating system software is meant to maintain and protect a computer's functionality, so from the designer's perspective, it serves a good purpose even though some may be cumbersome, time-consuming, and unpopular.

God created everything out of love and with the best intentions. Since life is a continuous cycle of evolution, there will be cycles of good and bad we will have to pass through. Nevertheless, the ultimate aim is always good because it is part of the original plan.

As we begin to understand this principle of energetic connections, we need to focus on raising our resonance level to higher vibrational frequencies. Let us consider a very simple example of the vibrational frequency in a home. Due to a lack of communication or a failure to complete energy conversions, the parents argue, fight, and shout whenever they are faced with problems, and the strong negative vibrations they create resonate throughout the house. These vibrational frequencies affect their children emotionally and psychologically and reshape their mindsets, and they may prompt aggressive behavior and violent impulses in the children.

On the other hand, if the parents are always calm and treat each other with love and respect, they generate a peaceful atmosphere in their home that positively influences their children's mindsets.

Economic crises can heavily influence our lives. The heaven-earth-human viewpoint, which can be translated into destiny, environment, and mind, can be used to analyze the situation. We observe the unstable economy and realize that it is a global problem that affects everybody and is driven by greed and selfishness. In many countries, political leaders and citizens are starting to recognize that the system has failed. Since these people live in environments that create trouble such as riots, unrest, and war, they must look for options to survive. When everyone falls off the cliff and reaches the bottom, all the people will be willing to change and will develop one mind about it.

When we fall off a cliff and hit bottom, we will learn the true essence of compassion, wisdom, and courage because failure and suffering can teach us the values of love and humility. This is a lesson we learned from the war in Vietnam. A rich and powerful man thought he had everything on earth, so he did not really care about how others suffered from hunger and poverty. When the country fell, he fled it. He struggled in the jungle without food and clothing because he had lost everything. He learned to love because of the poor strangers who shared their food and clothing with him and taught him to be humble.

When we fail at something or are suffering for any reason, we have to rely on everything we have learned to handle the situation or possibly to even survive it. As we look back, we see these difficult moments as memorable because they have affected our lives and have helped us develop wisdom and understanding. We can learn from our failures if we develop wisdom based on them. It is our human nature to survive; this ability is a built-in function of our brains. When we deal with failure and suffering, we tend to pull ourselves together and get through these tough times. For this reason, failure and suffering can strengthen our courage and determination or willpower. We can use the energy concept as a tool to maintain the balance of our energy especially when we are caught in the middle of life's storms. Eventually, after weathering many storms, we will discover the strength of our courage and determination.

We often hear the phrase "Failure is not an option." If we program that notion into our thinking process, it may create distractions and bring pressure and stress because we cannot be in control of the heaven-earth-human factors. We can plan for all possible scenarios including the worst, but we cannot predict what will happen in the next hour or the next minute, so how can we predict our destiny? We have no control over the heavenly timing factor. If we lock our minds on one view, that failure is not an option, we may have problems when failure is the only option.

When I lived in California, I loved to play American football, basketball, and tennis. Since I lived in San Jose during the 1980s, my favorite National Football League team was (and still is) the San Francisco 49ers. This team was transformed by Coach Bill Walsh (1931–2007). When he was hired as head coach in 1979, the team ended up with a dismal record of 2–14. They improved to 6–10 in 1980, and in 1981, they won the Super Bowl.[6] During the 1990s, I witnessed Michael Jordan carry his team, the Chicago Bulls, all the way to winning the NBA championship. When I learned to play tennis in the 1970s, it was only a baseline game, but when John McEnroe entered the Association of Tennis Professionals arena in

---

[6] https://www.encyclopedia.com/people/sports-and-games/sports-biographies/bill-walsh.

1978 with his serve-and-volley tactics, he added another dimension to the game. Despite adverse conditions and the odds against them, these athletes were able to focus and have a great impact on their sports. I use these examples to remind myself and my children that we can focus to face adversity, failure, obstacles, and problems and prevail with strength and determination. We may lose a battle, but we will win the war.

It is a two-way transaction between the humans and the divine beings. If we maintain our faith and place our trust in the divine beings, we are doing our part. Certainly, God and the divine beings can see exactly what we need to carry out our duties, and they will provide everything we need when we are ready. Many ask the divine beings and sometimes even challenge them to show them some signs or miracles to gain their trust. Others realize that we are profoundly fortunate to have been given the opportunity to learn. Our souls have not done anything to deserve this gift, so how can we even think of demanding signs and miracles? We should appreciate what the divine beings have given us and be more compassionate, conscious, responsible, and trustworthy at all times. Perhaps then, the people around us will benefit from that as well. I have learned to trust and work in divine instead of human timing.

With the capacity to convert negative energy into positive energy, we can learn how to fail with successful results. We anxiously await the transition that will bring the human race into a new era. Throughout history, there have been many predictions and much speculation about the state of the world in the near future. In the next paragraphs, we will address some of the negative and positive aspects of humanity's current state.

From a pessimistic point of view, the human race is heading toward annihilation. This is a valid projection to make as we logically look at the present condition of the world. Science has made great advancements, but they include weapons of mass destruction. The breakthroughs in medical science have given human beings the power to play God because we can alter genetic codes through cloning technology and experiment with viral mutations. Now, we suddenly find ourselves in real danger as we are forced to confront the deadly outcome of the errors we have made.

Since we want to play the role of the Creator, we must face all the consequences of our actions because we can neither control nor predict the widespread damage of unknown viruses. On top of that, the earth's environment is also affected by pollution and contamination of all sorts. From a scientific perspective, we are living in a world of decay, disease, danger, and death. From a social perspective, we live in an environment of total chaos. We have crime and corruption that range from the personal level up to the governmental level. The family, the basic unit of human society, is being completely ignored. As we look more deeply into our spiritual evolution, we see that we are facing a major problem and that we must change the way we are progressing.

With this rate of evolution, it takes a very long time for a soul to progress and eventually reach the divine level. We know it takes a long time for a soul to go through the cycle of reincarnation, to learn and evolve in this material world. Currently, as a soul comes down on this earth, it has to learn all aspects of life to complete its training and transcend to the level of a higher being. Souls must learn many lessons in the physical world to attain the state of divine love. We were born with constrained physical bodies, and we were heavily influenced by selfish love. Our parents planted seeds of selfish love in our minds though they cared for us as best they could, but our minds and hearts are trapped by their selfish love. We must learn to distinguish between selfish love and divine love. We have been influenced by family structures, educational programs, and social and religious systems, so most of us know how to express only selfish love. We can talk about love and compassion but not show it because we do not truly understand the definition of love. As we apply this idea, we are often blocked by our bodies and egos, so we express love only in selfish ways due to factors such as greed, lust, fame, fortune, and personal interest. As a result, we can see how difficult it is for a soul to progress since the rate of evolution is very slow. The condition of the physical world effectively blocks our paths when we try to learn true love—divine love.

From an optimistic point of view, there have been numerous predictions concerning the new earth, one where people live in peace and harmony. In this new system, the human race will know how to lead godly lives and the social structure will be built on the principle of divine love. We will learn to truly understand and support each other and enhance our spiritual development as well.

In a world of chaos and fear, we are constantly facing death and destruction. We can depend only on hope and perseverance to find the solution. During this critical period, the Creator has reached down to guide and enlighten us in a unique and profound way. It is a technique of meditation to maintain good health. It is also a method to help us enhance our spiritual development through practical application in real life. In fact, even though it includes meditation and health, this is actually a way that the Creator uses human beings to express divine love and exercise divine wisdom.

As mentioned above, since we are attached to our physical bodies, selfish love is the way we currently express ourselves and interact with others. This results in giving us a false sense of reality from which we can never break free to see the light of truth and transcend spiritually. Depending totally on our bodies restricts and sometimes halts our spiritual growth. The brain naturally filters information through the process of logical analysis, so the information can be pure and true, but as it enters the brain, it is distorted and judged to be either right or wrong, good or bad, valuable or worthless. As the information is filtered and distorted through this binary process, the message is transferred down to the rest of the body, which triggers a chain reaction that may cause many shock waves. For example, we may witness an act that is completely innocent and true, but our brains may interpret it as wrong or evil, and this chemically encoded message is carried to the cardiovascular system along with the other systems in the body. As a result, it causes acceleration of the heart rate and increased blood pressure and adrenaline levels. It can trigger stress and perhaps even violent rage beyond a person's control. The physical body will gradually wear down and get sick mentally as well as physically if it is regularly subjected to such shock waves.

## Selfish Love and Divine Love

Selfish love is the root of evil and suffering. Selfish love can manifest itself as greed, hatred, desire, and jealousy. It can turn strength into weakness, joy into torment, and sincerity into deception. Due to selfish love, we have fought and destroyed each other for reasons that have ranged from personal to racial differences, from social to religious ideologies, from economic to political domination, and from desire to obsession. Our souls are trapped because we are living in a world that can deliver only a false sense of reality and peace. Therefore, we must try to find a new concept, a new way, and a new world. To reach this objective, we have to erase everything we have learned in this material world. If we start cutting the ropes that bind our souls and block our spiritual progress, we will find ourselves looking at a new horizon of a new world—the spiritual realm.

Love is a force that can help us break our bonds, but it has to be the true love that God shines into our souls. As God plants the seed of true love in our hearts, He will nurture it for it to grow strong. Ultimately, it becomes the power that enables our souls to take control of our bodies. When that happens, our souls begin to reach into the strength of God and the seed He has planted grows and becomes divine love, and God will use its light to shine into the souls of others. Without this grace, the human soul will be trapped in a world of darkness forever because selfish love is the restraint that binds us on this earth. It also gives us a false sense of peace, one that inevitably causes us to lose trust in and sometimes even deny God. Armed with this awareness, we must leap forward to liberate ourselves from the darkness of selfish love so we can reach the light of divine love.

To define divine love, we need to disregard all references that link it to this physical world. We cannot describe divine love from a religious point of view or from the standards of the physical senses. Divine love has no limitations because it is the heart and spirit of God. It is the light as well as the strength of God that created everything. When we reach the level of divine love, we do not depend on the physical senses or logic and we do not judge anything. At this level, we recognize that good and evil, right and wrong are one. We learn and benefit from good and bad experiences alike. We look at everything from a much deeper perspective. We realize that everything happening is under God's control and that He has a purpose for every action. As a result, we learn to trust God and to see the way He reaches and enlightens us. Developing the ability to accept all things is one way for us to develop trust in God. As we reach more deeply into this trust, we will find the truth.

Eventually, on the path to find divine love, we will realize it requires total devotion on our part and our destiny, which is realized in the life God has designed for us. We can never reach divine love if we miss either of these two criteria. We must concentrate our efforts and spend our lives or our many lives to attain self-control so we can detach from the material world. That requires almost superhuman strength and effort. Even if we reach this goal, without God's grace, we will not grasp the profound meaning of our spiritual existence and never recognize our purpose and path.

I devoted my life to searching for the heart of God, divine love. On this journey, I had to start from a religious foundation that provided the basic principles and doctrines for me to set my course. With this focus, I had a direction to concentrate my training on and to improve myself. I had to learn the virtues to facilitate becoming a better person. There were many lessons in the practice of self-control—lessons about perseverance, diligence, discernment, obedience, sacrifice, and faith for instance. These virtues had one common principle—love and compassion. I slowly discovered that it was the path of love. However, if I still depend on this physical world to find divine love and continued to rely on myself and my virtues, I will reach a boundary that will stop my progress. This would happen because I would be forced to face reality—the constraints of the human capacity and the limitations of the physical world.

I have become more aware of the many wonders that existed beyond the physical world that the mind could never imagine. Only then did I understand that I had reached the boundary and that without God's assistance, I would never see the other side of the wall. Even if I tried my best to train and improve myself, I was still restricted by physical standards, so my training would never be complete. All I could find was my own definition of love, which was actually selfish love, because I knew how to express it only according to the ways of the world. Being trapped by the standards and precepts of the physical world, I suddenly realized how difficult and treacherous it was for souls to transcend and reach the hand of God. We had been trapped and had suffered for so long that it felt like eternal damnation, that there was no hope of escaping from the tight grip of this material world. Only God could break these chains and barriers to liberate our souls.

Through this act of divine grace, God will break everything in the material world. Through my own path, I realized that God had to break my happiness, dreams, hopes, and beliefs into pieces and that I had to face the death of my body.

God made sure I knew that everything I had built and tried to keep in this world could disappear in less than a second and that I could not do anything to prevent it. When I almost lost my life, I came to recognize the power and wisdom of God, who controls our lives, deaths, and destinies. God brings life to this world, and He can take life away.

Through this process, the human soul learns and reaches His divine love. God sends us to this earth to live and to learn, and He uses divine love to reach into the depths of our hearts and souls to pull us together and enlighten us. God will alter our lives as He reaches into the depths of our souls. We will experience the total transformation of our hearts through our perception of our expressions and actions. We will not analyze or comprehend things as normal human beings do and as we had done in the past. Instead, we will begin to think in a godly manner. In this way, we will have very clear vision since we will not be blocking our views with distractions such as judgment, emotions, and ego. We will no longer feel like using human emotions or love from the physical heart. Rather, we will begin to sense and express true love from the inner soul—divine love. Eventually, God will transform our lives so we can serve as lights of divine love that will shine into the hearts of people to pull them closer to Him. Also, we will represent the strength of trusting in God to guide and help all human souls to enhance their spiritual growth.

Human souls have been trapped in this material world for so long that they are blocking the evolutionary progress of other souls. The first time that we reached the level of human beings, we were born onto this earth with all the material temptations and distractions. We were deceived by all the beauties and wonders of this world. We totally forgot our main purpose, which was and still is to use this material world as the means to learn and progress from one life to the next. We were lost and stuck in this material world. We held on so tightly to this earth and its belongings because we thought we had found everything we needed here.

If we understand and put into practice an idea or concept from divine wisdom, we may progress many steps on our path of evolution. We can use the example of downloading data as a reminder of this. Let us say we search the internet for an app we need, download it, and install it on our computer so we can use it; we don't just download it and let it sit there as only a file. Similarly, when we hear profound advice but let it go in one ear and out the other, nothing is recorded. It is the same as a data file we have simply stored on our hard disk. However, if we apply profound words of advice to our lives, we will see a myriad possibilities of our development and experience personal transformation.

We can use the expression "full of hot air" to elaborate on the concept of an energy transfer. If we attempt a conversation simply to boast, gossip, or judge others, that is due to a selfish motive. We are transmitting sound waves that do not carry any positive effect, and in most cases, they are empty words that fade away. Most of us have heard people trying to impress others by boasting for example. We did not pay much attention to it and immediately forgot what they were saying. From the perspective of the energy transfer, this person wasted time and effort to transmit sound waves that quickly faded. If we raise our levels of consciousness enough, we will recognize such energy losses, failed communications, and wasted time. As we learn to correct these mistakes, we begin to improve ourselves.

If we learn from our failures in the material world, we will not repeat them and we will succeed spiritually. The road ahead will be better because we will have favorable, not adverse circumstances and will have all the elements working for us rather than against us. We will have the benefits of heavenly timing in which all spiritual beings assist us and cause an event to happen at the precise moment when it can make the most impact. We will have the earthly advantage wherein the resources will be available for us to be very efficient. We will have human harmony in which the people we need can work together productively.

When we accidentally download a virus, we have to update our antivirus software to fix that. Likewise, we need updated maps when we are driving someplace unfamiliar so we can avoid delays and unnecessary detours. If we learn from our failures and mistakes and try to change our thinking processes and behaviors, we will benefit from seemingly bad situations, avoid making mistakes, and harvest golden opportunities.

## Chapter 27
# RETURNING FROM THE GRAVE

No legal system, political authority, financial power, scientific technology, or intellectual prowess can stop the angel of death from taking our lives; only God can do that. However, some people who met the angel of death witnessed the divine grace as God gave them another chance to live. Those who have had near-death experiences have changed their perspectives and lifestyles. With our physical eyes, we cannot see what is coming around the corner. We can be in an awful or tragic situation, but we should think of God's mercy and what may lie around the corner. I cried out and blamed God for allowing the most tragic event to happen to me when I was in pain. Many years later, I also cried out with the deep feeling of gratitude and a tremendous sense of guilt because God had blessed me with a beautiful family. Many have taken a similar journey and share the same sentiment. This is a testimony of God's wonderful hands as He planted the seeds of resiliency in the fertile field of my life.

Through the years, God had transformed my tears of sorrow into tears of joy, and the seeds of resiliency are growing strong and healthy. God, a magnificent farmer, works wonders with any field whether it is fertile or rocky. He has given us all unique seeds, latent abilities, that need to germinate at the right depth and be irrigated properly. During their infancy, the seeds need nutrition and protection. In their adolescence, they need guidance and support. When they fully mature, they will be exposed to different environments and interact with others.

Some people lost faith in God when they were buried in many layers of challenges, disappointments, problems, suffering, and trials. Their hearts turned cold and their minds became skeptical. These are tough seeds, and after germination, they will grow strong. I share my story as an encouraging sign, and I hope they can tap into the collective knowledge base to see God's grace and wisdom. These words are meaningless without actual testimonies and more important the invisible hands of God, who turns them into actionable learning opportunities in each person's situation.

Since I have gone through turbulent storms and found hidden potential in God's grace, I pray for difficult trials. I trust God to bring rain and sunshine alike to promote growth in every living creature. I appreciate the fact that God allows me to be tested, and I thank Him for reaching His graceful hands to guide me through those storms.

As I went through one storm to another, my bond with God grew stronger and my faith became unshakable. My challenges boosted my capabilities and consequently made me stronger. This is the idea of the vitamins of the fruits of failure, disappointment, and suffering as mentioned earlier.

## Chapter 28
# MY SUBMISSIVE SON STORY

I was born and raised in a country that was heavily influenced by cultural rules, social standards, family traditions, and religious doctrines. I was raised to be a filial son and a righteous person. I learned to obey my parents, teachers, religious leaders, and government officials. I was to be obedient and submissive at home, in school, and in public. Being raised and educated in this social and family environment, I was programmed to be obedient and not challenge authority. I learned to discipline myself to obey rather than oppose and to adapt rather than challenge.

My father was a dominant figure who set rules for me that I had to follow or eventually be disowned by him. As an air force officer, my father had a high level of self-discipline. He expected his children to always do the best they could.

My submissive attitude was fine when I was growing up and single; it did not cause any issues between my father and me. But when I was married, I was no longer an individual; I was part of a unit that included my wife and children. When I did not speak up or stand up for my family, I lost my wife's confidence in me. I wanted to be neutral and avoid confrontation not to disappoint my father. As a result, I lost my father as well as my wife because of my weakness. That was a tough lesson to learn. God arranged such difficult circumstances to teach me, and when I learned the lesson, I realized His good intentions.

I did not impose too many conditions on my children. I love them and respect their decisions. The energy I spent on my children will come back to me. They will remember what I passed on to them and maintain connections with me due to our energetic bond, which will help them navigate difficult times in their lives.

I was submissive to my father due to cultural, traditional, familial, and societal pressures. By being submissive to the heavenly Father, I learned many good lessons and had opportunities that allowed me to reach beyond those limitations. God has been working behind the scenes to help me reconcile with my father and family. Through my mistakes and failures as a submissive son, I have confirmed that we should be submissive and trust God, who always plans or allows something to happen for our benefit even though it might be a tough challenge or a difficult trial.

*Chapter 29*

# MY DISHWASHER STORY

One day, my wife asked me and our children if they noticed a smell in the kitchen. We said we did not, but she was sure she smelled something. She determined it was coming from the dishwasher. She checked it out and discovered that food particles had clogged up the lower spray arms. After cleaning them out and running the dishwasher, the smell was gone. She had noticed a problem though no one else had, and she had addressed it successfully.

We are going through an unprecedented problem with the coronavirus; some people did not recognize the severity of the pandemic at first but eventually faced reality. Those who recognized the problem proposed different solutions based on their differing economic, political, and scientific perspectives. If we cannot work together for the benefits of the entire human race, problems will continue to vex us and get worse. It is a challenge to acknowledge and identify problems, and it is even tougher to confront and find win-win solutions. We can work together to identity and solve problems when we have open minds, truthful and humble attitudes, mutual respect, compassion, wisdom, and courage.

We may have challenging and difficult problems, but we can endure and learn from them and become stronger and wiser. Elizabeth Smart was abducted in June 2002 when she was fourteen. She endured months of abuse until she was rescued in March 2003. She became stronger, and more important, she shared her experiences to encourage and help others overcome their problems. Her book *My*

*Story* contains many inspirational and profound messages, and this one is my favorite.

> Some of my own ancestors were early pioneers. They faced suffering and starvation, the loss of their children, the loss of other loved ones. They too endured the gamut of emotions, from utter devastation to lifesaving miracles. But the human spirit is resilient. God made us so. He gave us the ability to forgive. To leave our past behind. To look forward instead of back. I'm not the first one who has ever done this. People have been doing it for generations. Since the beginning of time, men have found ways to heal. (Smart, 299)

Hien Pham traveled with Dr. Ravi Zacharias in 1971 to military bases and hospitals and prisons during the Vietnam War. Dr. Zacharias was invited to speak and spread the gospel, and Hien was his interpreter. Dr. Zacharias left Vietnam in 1971, and many years later, they met again in the United States. This is Hien Pham's incredible story of faith that Dr. Zacharias wrote about in his book *Walking from East to West.*

> After Vietnam fell, Hien was captured by the Vietcong and imprisoned. They accused him of collaborating with the CIA, since he had worked with missionaries. In prison, they worked him over, telling him again and again that he had been brainwashed by Westerners. They took away his Bible and forbade him to speak English, the language he had loved, permitting him to use only Vietnamese or French.

> "There is no such thing as God," came the refrain from his captors, day after hellish day.

The hour finally came when Hien wondered, "Maybe they are right. Maybe there is no such thing as God." As he thought back to some of my sermons and the shared blessings we had enjoyed, he wondered if perhaps I had been deluded too. That night he went to bed, muttering to himself, "I'm through with God. When I wake up in the morning, no more God, no more prayer."

The new day dawned, and the commanding officer of the prison barked out the assignments for the day. Hien was to clean the latrines. He cringed when he heard it. It was the ultimate form of indignity for the prisoners. The latrines were the absolute dregs of human filth, and Hien spent the entire day in those inhospitable surroundings.

His final task was to empty the trash cans, which were filled with soiled toilet paper. All day long, he labored with reminders to himself—"No God today." But as his work was coming to an end, something in the last trash can happened to catch his eye. It was a piece of paper with printed type. As Hien looked closer, he saw it was in English. Hungry to read this language again, he looked around to make sure nobody was watching. He hastily rinsed off the filth and tucked the paper into his pocket.

That night, after everyone had fallen asleep, he carefully took out his flashlight and removed the still damped paper from his pocket. In the upper right-hand corner of the page were the words "Romans 8."

The Bible.

Hien, in a state of shock, began reading.

"And now we know that in all things God works for the good of those who love him, who have been called according to his purpose."

He read on.

"What, then, shall we say in response to this? If God is for us, who can be against us? … For I am convinced that neither death nor life, neither angels or demons, neither the present nor the future, nor any powers, neither height nor depth, nor anything else in all creation, will be able to separate us from the love of God that is in Christ Jesus our Lord."

Hien began crying. Of all the Scripture verses he had known, these were the ones he most needed to hear, and now they had come back to him. "Lord," he realized, "you would not let me out of your reach for even one day." He turned over in his bed that night and prayed.

The next morning, when he saw the commanding officer, Hien asked him, "Sir, would you mind if I cleaned the latrines again?"

The officer stared at him, quite puzzle. Thinking Hien was being rather arrogant, he decided to assign him to the latrines indefinitely. "You are going to clean them everyday, until I tell you to stop," he commanded.

Hien did not know it in the beginning, but the officer himself had been tearing out those pages from the

Bible and using them for toilet paper. Now, each day, Hien rinsed them clean, hid them in his pocket, and used them for this devotion at night. He ended up collecting numerous passages from the book of Romans, as well as from other books of the Bible ...

Eventually, he made it to San Francisco, and, after earning a degree from the University of California (Berkeley), he now ran a financial planning firm. (Zacharias, 218–20).

PART IX

# Chapter 30
# BEING IN LINE WITH THE DIVINE WILL

Whenever I am in a dark storm or facing adverse situation and difficult problems, I remind myself of the divine will. I have learned the links between losses, failures, and trials and compassion, wisdom, and courage. My failures taught me the value of humility and gave me wisdom. The difficult trials became the vitamins that gradually boosted my courage.

In the beginning, before I understood the divine will, my life's storms caused me tremendous suffering, but as I went through one storm after another, I began to see a pattern. The drop that filled the cup was the car crash I had been in that brought me to face the divine will. From that moment on, I constantly observed and tried to be in line with the divine will.

We live in a very unstable environment though on the surface everything seems to be normal. A number of people actually know we are in a very dangerous time since they are directly involved in or responsible for the causes. I see the art of resiliency as a tool to deal with storms by understanding the chain of events and adapting or coping better.

Those who use computers have their own ways of accessing and updating data on the networks they are connected to. All users have to work with the network's operating system (OS) because it controls data structure, database management, and user authority. It is important that each user knows the OS and follows its guidelines to minimize glitches and issues. When there is an error or problem, the OS will take corrective measures and its users will gain some understanding of how the OS works. I learned through my many mistakes to recognize how the divine will (or OS) worked and to trust it more than my instincts. Eventually, I integrated my thinking process with the divine will, and my will became a part of the divine will. Our main purpose in life should be to learn about and follow the divine will so our journey will have heavenly timing, earthly advantage, and human harmony.

In *The Analects*, Confucius gave us a general guideline for focusing on our life journey.

> At fifteen, I had my mind bent on learning.
> At thirty, I stood firm.
> At forty, I had no doubts.
> At fifty, I knew the decrees of Heaven.
> At sixty, my ear was an obedient organ for the reception of truth.
> At seventy, I could follow what my heart desired, without transgressing what was right.
> (Legge, 1893, 2:4)

Two causes of aggression, conflict, destruction, suffering, and war are selfishness and power struggles. In Friedrich Max Müller's translation of *The Dhammapada*, one of the most famous Buddhist scriptures, we read, "From greed comes grief, from greed comes fear; he who is free from greed knows neither grief nor fear" (Müller, chapter 17, verse 216) and "Let a man leave anger, let him forsake pride, let him overcome all bondage! No sufferings befall the man who is not attached to name and form, and who calls nothing his own" (Müller, chapter 17, verse 221). We have this advice from Jesus Christ: "Take care, and be on your guard against all covetousness, for one's life does not consist in the abundance of his possessions" (Luke 12:15 ESV). Here is another good reminder: "For where jealousy and selfish ambition exist, there will be disorder and every vile practice" (James 3:16 ESV).

A way to effectively deal with the selfishness virus and the power virus is to learn to control our cravings. Here is a beautiful and profound message I received during one morning meditation.

> Focus diligently to see each life event as a tiny drop of blessing, even when you are in a turbulent storm. As you develop the strength of resiliency, you will have a large bucket of blessings. Eventually, you will benefit from the greatest blessing of all as you become one with the Divine Will. At that point, your path will always have favorable conditions since you no longer have obstacles or problems because you see them as hidden blessings that will be realized further down the road.

Developing resiliency can help us gain a better understanding of the divine will. This approach involves self-cultivation by which we develop compassion, wisdom, and courage so we can take advantage of heavenly timing, earthly advantage, and human harmony. When we know and understand the divine will, the cosmic design specification, we can work with its objectives, and this is a reciprocal relationship. We read in *A Source Book in Chinese Philosophy* that Mo Tzu said, "When I do what Heaven wants, Heaven also does what I want" (Chan, 218). We can all achieve this goal with God's assistance, which He gives to all His children as a merciful, responsible, and wise parent.

## Chapter 31
# PRACTICALITY, EFFICIENCY, TRUST, AND POSITIVENESS

We can adapt the practicality, efficiency, trust, and positiveness factors in our thinking process. We can remind ourselves that our thoughts, words, and actions should be practical, efficient, trustworthy, and positive. If a thought, word, or deed satisfies the framework of these four variables, we can proceed whether we are in a good or a bad situation. Especially when we are in bad situations, this equation can help us reexamine and look at the bright side of all things.

When we do something, we should remind ourselves that if the concept or idea is practical and the process is efficient, the chance of failing is minimal. At the human level, trust is very important; with trust, people can work and support each other to develop collective strength and unbreakable bonds. From an energetic perspective, positiveness brings confidence and enhances unity within people, families, and organizations. Positive thinking will produce positive outcomes and not let negative circumstances cause us to be negative. We should add a practicality, efficiency, trust, and positiveness checklist to our brain's operating system because when we have these four factors, we will not fail.

These words and ideas may sound good, but they are not easy to apply because we need commitment and discipline. During our daily routines, we are easily distracted and influenced by material factors such as tradition, culture, society, and family. Therefore, our thinking process may be clumsy, unreasonable, unstable, and skeptical. We constantly deal with external challenges and adversity; these may include business competition, economic crises, political pressure, and religious influences that discourage us. We also have internal challenges and adversity from a variety of sources such as family issues, conflicts with colleagues, and other relationship problems. These factors can cause divisions that can eventually cause us to fall apart. We also have circumstantial and personal challenges such as our egos, emotions, and mentalities that can ruin and even destroy us.

We can discipline our bodies and minds by learning who we really are, which means discovering our true selves, which can control our egos and the sources of distractions including doubt, fear, greed, hatred, and jealousy.

Meditation can help us discover our true selves; it is a continual process by which we attempt to attain harmony between the body and the soul. The physical body has ambitions, desires, and goals, but the soul definitely knows its purpose. If body and soul reach a sufficient level of harmony, the soul will be in control and can use the body in an efficient, practical, trustworthy, and positive manner, which will enable it to accomplish its mission. We are looking at the will of the body and the will of the soul, which is a part of God's will. Our will cannot be firm because it is constantly affected by material and spiritual factors; thus, we have anguish, confusion, contradictions, doubts, and fears. God's will is trustworthy and unshakable because it overrides all material and spiritual factors, and thus, we gain clarity, confidence, courage, and peace. But we need to have total discipline in order to follow God's will.

When we are learning and focusing on an inner search, we begin to look at everything from a deeper perspective. We will eventually see beyond a person's outer self or physical appearance and look at a person's inner self or soul because we are focusing on the signs, the reasons for an event rather than what it is.

When we learn to develop a positive mindset and apply it in our daily routines, we can change our perception to always look on the bright side of everything. The Buddhist concept of the footstep of flowers refers to the legend that lotus flowers sprang up in the footprints left by the Buddha after His birth.[7] With a positive mindset, our thoughts and actions are conscious because they come from our true love and our sincere hearts. Consequently, we radiate the energy of joy and peace that can make an impact at home and in school, our work places, and our communities. Directly or indirectly, we thus plant seeds of happiness and tolerance that will eventually blossom.

Following the energy approach, we have the ability to radiate the light of God's presence. First, we need to train and develop the GPE in us by going through the process of purification and self-realization so we will achieve harmony between body and soul. After we reach a certain GPE level, we need to maintain it as best we can. Some of us have discovered that after we manage to have a high GPE level for a day, we feel happy and peaceful. However, the next day, we might face challenges and difficulties that cause our GPE level to drop, and we fall back to struggle and suffer in the darkness again. Eventually, through many ordeals during which our GPE level fluctuates, we become accustomed to handling sudden changes, and as a result, these experiences shed some light for us. Although we try to use words to describe this profound concept, it ultimately depends on our perception to grasp the idea.

When we can constantly maintain our GPE level, the next step is to let it shine and affect those around us starting with our families and expanding to others in our many environments. We will transfer our positive energy vibrations to them through our thoughts, words, and actions. Matches can start a fire, but a blowtorch makes that task so much easier particularly under adverse conditions such as on a rainy or windy day. We can use this example as a reminder when we try to generate the light of joy to help ourselves and others.

---

[7] https://www.bbc.co.uk/teach/life-of-the-buddha-a-spiritual-journey/zjf4y9q.

## Chapter 32
# THE POINT OF NO RETURN

Another related idea for us to contemplate is the notion of the point of no return. There are three views that we can draw from this concept—the reaction time, the attracting force, and the radiating effect.

**Reaction Time:** When we are driving and the light turns yellow, we have to decide if we are beyond the point of no return and thus drive through the intersection or if we are short of the point of no return and step on the brakes. When we realize that we have reached the point of no return, we rule out doubt and hesitation and become brave, confident, and determined to make it through.

**The Attracting Force:** Let us imagine being in a spacecraft that is returning to earth that has come under the effects of gravity; we cannot escape that force, so we become totally focused on just landing; we make the best out of an inevitable situation.

**The Radiating Effect:** If we visit an area that has undergone a nuclear disaster area, we know our bodies will be exposed to increasing levels of radiation the closer we get to ground zero. We realize that we are getting too attached or involved in a situation that will eventually affect us to greater and greater degrees.

We can also use the scenario of the Christmas season to illustrate the idea of the point of no return. During September and October, we do not think of Christmas shopping, but in December, we begin to feel pressure to go shopping. We might put it off because we are busy with work and other concerns, but during the last week before Christmas, we realize that we cannot put off buying gifts any longer.

We are drawn to all the available gift ideas as we work down our Christmas shopping list.

During Christmas, we will frequently see nativity scenes on TV or at church; they are reminders that we are to keep in step with the divine will so we can receive God's guidance.

Christians who start off their days with praying can maintain their connection to and focus on God throughout the day and have a better understanding of how events of the day unfold. This is hard to do consistently especially through daily ups and downs. One reason for this is that most of us do not like to hear and accept the Word of truth because it means we have to change our lifestyles, habits, careers, and even our futures. Perhaps in the past we prayed and asked for certain favors but did not receive answers to our prayers and we began to lose faith. If we look only for material favors such as fame and money, we may not see the dangers or potential complications such favors come with. God, however, already knows what lies ahead, and being a responsible parent, He would not give us something harmful to our growth. When we become more mature spiritually, we will develop a better perspective and understanding especially at the moment we have to face reality. It may be bitter or painful in the beginning to swallow the Word of Truth, but gradually, we will see it start to work.

The subject of making a positive impact also came up from those conversations. Here, we include questions that will enter our minds at the end of our journey—What was my life's purpose? Did I fulfill it? Now can I help my soul? What do I leave behind? What have I done in this lifetime? It is as though we are watching a movie of the significant moments in our lives. If all we see are our normal routines such as getting up in the morning, going to work, going back home day after day, month after month, year after year until this moment, we realize that we have lived but had not had a life. We were living by the clock just like a machine operating with its normal functions such as eating, sleeping, working, and playing. We were trapped by material constraints. We may have accomplished something in the material world, for instance, saving a lot of money, buying a big house, and so on, but we realize that three months after we die, everything we have spent our lives accomplishing will mean nothing.

If we focus on making an impact only on the physical world, we will be constantly affected and influenced by material factors such as tradition, culture, family, and society. We will be operating within the vibrational frequencies that tend to have negative influences such as anger, doubt, fear, greed, and jealousy. We can measure the impact we have made in life when we reflect on whether we created negativity such as chaos, conflict, confusion, destruction, hostility, hurt, and separation or if we generated positive effects such as harmony, joy, love, peace, trust, and wisdom to everyone. After we are gone, when people think of us, will they have good or bad memories of us? Will we have left behind a positive or negative impression?

Let us consider the concepts of physical energy and spiritual energy. Physical energy is limited in its influence because it is bound by space and time and can be disrupted by interferences, weakened by distance, and subjected to fading over time. We might be able to carry a hundred kilograms for a hundred meters if we are not distracted, but we will become exhausted if we try to exceed our capabilities and our energy will fade.

Spiritual energy on the other hand is connected to our levels of consciousness and capacity. Here, we are talking about our ability to comprehend the causes and effects of everything that happens around us and our ability to influence our surroundings. We can grasp this point by referring to what Jesus said: "Heaven and earth will pass away, but my words will not pass away" (Luke 21:33 ESV). We may relate to this idea more easily when we try to express ourselves or say something, but the words can get lost in the midst of surrounding noises or disappear as soon as they come out of our mouths. Sometimes, they simply fade away in a few days and we cannot even remember what we said. With our ordinary levels of focus and consciousness, we do not have sufficient capacity to reach beyond the thick cloud layer of physical energy, which includes a variety of factors such as doubt, emotion, fear, greed, hatred, jealousy, sickness, space, and time. Jesus was definitely not talking about the words in the contexts of the physical realm because He made it clear that His kingdom was "not of this world" (John 18:36 ESV). His focus and thus His energy vibration operated on a higher level, so His words were not affected by space and time in the physical realm.

As our physical energy lessens as we get older, our biochemical system may cease functioning properly and we will start experiencing problems with our eyes, ears, joints, and muscles. This represents one range of energy frequency. The higher range is the spiritual energy, which can potentially help us in many aspects. With a higher state of consciousness, we can help optimize the functions of this biochemical system to maintain our health. If we synchronize ourselves with the higher vibration, i.e., cosmic energy, we can overcome the disturbances and interference coming from the lower wavelengths in the material world such as anger, anxiety, conflict, selfishness, and treachery. With this higher level of focus, we are using spiritual energy and the vibrations that can make a long and lasting impact. Jesus's words have lasted more than two thousand years and continue to affect people's lives. We need to learn from this example and not send out empty words or blow bubbles that disappear immediately or fade away. When we say anything, we should really believe it and live it. What we express from our hearts is more important than what we express from our brains.

Regarding the values of the heart and talent, I share the profound words from *The Tale of Kiều* (*Truyện Kiều* in Vietnamese) written by Nguyễn Du (1766–1820). I have translated them almost word for word to keep as my personal reminder.

> Đã mang lấy nghiệp vào thân,
> Thì đừng trách lẫn Trời gần Trời xa.
> Thiện căn ở tại lòng ta,
> Chữ Tâm kia mới bằng ba chữ Tài.
> (verses 3249–3252)

> We brought karma upon ourselves,
> Do not blame God for being near or far.

The root of goodness lies within us,
The Heart is equal to three Talents.

God chose my wife to give me inspiration and strength. She can encourage me or break me down. She could push all my buttons to test me, but because of her love for me, she does that only to point out my flaws and weaknesses so I can handle tough situations better. During many discussions, she has asked me, "What is the moral of the story? What are you trying to say?" With my wife's questions, I wish to convey this message: *The Art of Resiliency*'s primary aim is to remind everyone of God's grace and love and that the main purpose of our lives should be to open our hearts and minds to find God's presence, and we need truthfulness and humility to do that.

Light the candle of God's presence in your heart and mind and maintain it in your daily routines; eventually, it will shine for all to see. The tiny candle of God's presence in your heart and mind will become a torch that will spark the fire of compassion, wisdom, and courage in the people around you.

When I received instructions to write this book many years ago, I knew God would use it as a tiny piece of burning ash from His flame that would light candles in others' hearts and minds. I share with you one of my favorite verses our Lord Jesus Christ left to remind us.

> You are the light of the world. A city set on a hill cannot be hidden. Nor do people light a lamp and put it under a basket, but on a stand, and it gives light to all in the house. In the same way, let your light shine before others, so that they may see your good works and give glory to your Father who is in heaven. (Matthew 5:14–16 ESV)

# References

Adels, Jill Haak. *Wisdom of the Saints: An Anthology.* Oxford University Press, 1989.

Chan, Wing-Tsit. *A Source Book in Chinese Philosophy,* Princeton University Press, 1969.

Frankl, Viktor. *Man's Search for Meaning.* Beacon Press, 2006.

"Galileo." *Biography.com,* A&E Networks Television, 4 Sept. 2019, www.biography.com/scholar/galileo.

Giles, Lionel, trans. *Sun Tzu on the Art of War.* Allandale Online Publishing, 2000.

"Joan of Arc." *Biography.com,* A&E Networks Television, 18 Apr. 2019, www.biography.com/military-figure/joan-of-arc.

Legge, James, trans. *The Analects of Confucius.* Clarendon Press, 1893.

Müller, Friedrich Max. *The Dhammapada.* Oxford, Clarendon Press, 1881.

Phan Thi, Kim Phuc. *Fire Road: the Napalm Girl's Journey through the Horrors of War to Faith, Forgiveness, and Peace.* Tyndale Momentum, 2017.

Smart, Elizabeth. *My Story.* St. Martin's Press, 2013.

*Spiritual Diary: Selected Sayings and Examples of Saints.* St. Paul Books and Media, 1990.

*The Holy Bible.* English Standard Version (ESV). The Gideons International, 2013.

Tran, Hoi B. *A Vietnamese Fighter Pilot in an American War.* Xlibris, 2011.

Zacharias, Ravi. *Walking from East to West.* Zondervan, 2006.